NARROW GAUGE
BY THE SUDANESE RED SEA COAST

THE TOKAR–TRINKITAT LIGHT RAILWAY
AND OTHER SMALL RAILWAYS

by

Henry Gunston

Published by
PLATEWAY PRESS
Taverner House, Harling Road
East Harling, Norfolk, England

Printed by
Postprint, East Harling, Norfolk, England

Front cover illustration: Hawthorn Leslie SR 56 heads a train of seed cotton bales across typical salt-flat scrub country. The original cab has been modified to Walter Ellis' requirements, and the first vehicle is the special brake wagon, adapted from a "D" class. The driver's assistant operated the hand brake wheel on the pillar on the front bogie. The vertical stanchions were inset from the ends, reducing the bale load to eighteen. The next five wagons have centre wells, so were almost certainly "F" class.

Frontispiece: Two Railway Tickets for Passengers on Tokar Light-Railway. No. 0001 Tokar to Trinkitat (Port) and No. 0001 Trinkitat to Tokar. Issued to Mrs K. F. Ellis, Wife of the General Manager of the TTLR. The first Passenger ever to travel on this Light-Railway. Fare 100 Milliemes or Ten Piastres equal to 2/- or 10 pence in 1978 money.

CONTENTS

DEDICATION

*This book is dedicated to David Ellis and
to the memory of Arthur and Walter Ellis
and Richard Hill*

PREFACE

The starting point of this book was a collection of photographs of a little-known 600mm gauge railway which once ran between Trinkitat, a small port on the Red Sea coast of the Sudan, and Tokar, the centre of an important cotton growing area. The photographic collection belonged to David Ellis, whose grandfather Arthur had been one of the two contractors who built the Tokar–Trinkitat Light Railway (TTLR) in the 1920s. Arthur Ellis managed the railway into the 1930s, firstly with his partner Mr Vincent, and later by himself. In 1930 Arthur was joined by his son Walter (David's father), fresh from completing his engineering apprenticeship with J. & H. McLaren of Leeds. Walter stayed on to help Arthur operate the TTLR until 1936, when the line became more closely controlled by Sudan Railways (SR), operators of the major network of 3ft 6in. gauge railways across the Sudan. The TTLR closed in 1952.

Although my own experiences with railways in Africa have mainly been in Kenya, Tanzania and Uganda, I was happy to be invited by Keith Taylorson to prepare a text to accompany publication of some of the photographs from the Ellis collection. Since that time, the project has been carried forward with enthusiasm by Plateway Press, especially by Sophie Lee, Andrew Neale and Jeremy Warren.

As my researches proceeded, it seemed relevant to explore not only the 18in gauge military railway from Trinkitat which preceded the TTLR, but also three other narrow gauge lines which were built near to the Sudanese Red Sea coast. These were at a military system at the port of Suakin, a public works railway to clear sand dunes around Tokar and an internal port railway at Port Sudan.

The remarkable collection of photographs and notes by members of the Ellis family form the core of the book, and my particular thanks go to David Ellis for his interest and support. I have also welcomed the encouragement and help of David Brewer, David Hall, the late Richard Hill, David Holroyde, Alan Merrells, Keith Taylorson, Rodney Weaver and C. R. Williams. A second major source of research material has been the Sudan Archive at the University of Durham, where Lesley Forbes and Jane Hogan provided much assistance. Help on particular queries has come from Allan C. Baker, Derek Bayliss, Colin J. Bruce (Imperial War Museum), Mike Cunningham, Dr H. R. J. Davies (University of Wales, Swansea), Chris Fisher, the archives of Hydrographer to the Navy, Lance King, Eric Maxwell, the Public Record Office, Mark Smithers, Christopher Veitch, Dr Linda Washington (National Army Museum), and Sue Wharton (Librarian, Institute of Hydrology). My thanks to them, and to any other contributors whose names I may have accidentally omitted.

In addition to the Ellis collection, I have relied heavily on writings and photographs from four former Sudan railwaymen:

■ The book "Sudan Transport, a history of railway marine and river services in the Republic of Sudan", by Richard Hill, published in 1965. This is the "standard work" on Sudanese transport history, and was the starting point of my own interests in the Sudan railway system in general, and the TTLR in particular. Mr Hill combined working for many years in the Traffic Department of Sudan Railways with a wide ranging interest in the history of the Sudan. His recent death was a great loss to Sudanese historical scholarship.

■ An article on the TTLR by D. L. Sharp in "The Sudan Railways Bulletin" No. 81, September 1945, made available by the Sudan Archive at the University of Durham. Mr Sharp retired in 1945 from the Sudan Railways post of Controller, TTLR.

■ Notes by G. R. Storrar on the planning and development of the TTLR in the early 1920s, from his diaries of the time, also made available by the Sudan Archive. Mr Storrar was Acting Chief (civil) Engineer of the SR in 1918, and Chief Engineer in 1926/27.

■ Notes on the TTLR in "Wheels and paddles in the Sudan 1923 – 1946", memories of a long career working for Sudan Railways by C. R. Williams, published in 1986. After some years on the mechanical engineering side, Mr Williams became Deputy General Manager of the SR during 1939–41, and General Manager during 1941–46.

A full list of the sources which I have consulted appears at the end of the book. For simplicity, these sources are referred to in the text (after the first entry) by the surname of their contributor, with exception of the use of the Christian names of Arthur, Walter and David Ellis.

The majority of photographs used in the book come from the Ellis collection. I would like to thank Allan C. Baker for providing the Bagnall locomotive illustrations of page 43, and the Sudan Archive at the University of Durham for permission to use the photos from the Tokar Sand Clearance Album which appear on pages 38, 39, 40, 57 (lower) and 59 and from the Storrar collection on page 10.

Exploring the stories of five narrow gauge railways described here has been a fascinating research exercise. One particular high-spot was the discovery (following considerable detective work, and aided by Jane Hogan of the Sudan Archive) that the Tokar Sand Clearance railway had been created by the Sudan Public Works Department. Another was the discovery that not even the remoter corners of the Sudan escaped the attention of Sir Felix J. C. Pole during his reign at Paddington as General Manager of the Great Western Railway! I hope that you enjoy reading the history of these small, but fascinating railways as much as I have enjoyed writing it.

Henry Gunston, Wantage, Oxfordshire, England,
December 2000

INTRODUCTION

"It was not at first sight a promising route for any kind of railway. The jetty at Trinkitat commanded only twelve feet of water, the harbour lacked fresh water which had to be brought from Suakin, and the terrain was so unstable and wind-blown that anything up to 60,000 cubic metres of sand dunes had to be shovelled from the track each year before trains could run."

Richard Hill "Sudan Transport"

The Sudan is a vast country. It has a land area of nearly a million square miles – more than ten times that of England, Scotland and Wales combined – much of it covered by sand dunes and barren, rocky semi-desert. However, we are concerned here not with the vastness of the Sudan but with a local area by its Red Sea coast, and especially with two short railways which ran inland from the small port of Trinkitat. The terminus of the first railway was at El Teb, the site of water wells and a small garrison fort – the scene of fierce fighting between Sudanese and Egyptian forces in 1883/84. The second railway ran further inland to Tokar, a town which was the centre of a rich agricultural district where the main commercial crop was cotton. In summary, the two railways from Trinkitat were:

a) an 18in. gauge line which ran for some 7ml. to water wells at El Teb, built in 1896 under Egyptian military supervision, but later abandoned;

b) the Tokar-Trinkitat Light Railway, a 600mm. gauge line some 20ml. long, primarily used for the export of the cotton crop from Tokar, built in 1921/22 by contractors, effectively absorbed by Sudan Railways in 1933, and closed in 1952.

The 600mm gauge line occupied the trackbed of the abandoned 18in. gauge railway from Trinkitat as far as El Teb, beyond which it took a fresh route onwards to Tokar. The precise name by which the 18in. gauge line was known is not clear. It will be referred to simply as the "18 inch gauge military railway to El Teb". The name "Tokar-Trinkitat Light Railway" (TTLR for short) applies only to the later 600mm. gauge line.

Extensive cotton growing in the Tokar delta area was first championed in 1865 by Ahmad Mumtaz Pasha, Turkish Governor of the region at that time, and there were early plans for rail transport to the Red Sea coast. "In 1871," as Richard Hill noted, "Shahin Bey Genj, whom the Khedive Ismail [the Turkish ruler of Egypt and parts of the Sudan] sent to inspect the Mumtaz Pasha's schemes, visited Tokar and recommended the construction of a jetty at Trinkitat and the laying of a railway to link it with the delta."

To set the broader geographical scene, some 40ml. north of Trinkitat lay Suakin, one of the oldest Red Sea ports. It was a centre of seaborne trade in the Red Sea region long before the coming of the Suez Canal, freight being carried in various sizes of that distinctive Arab sailing vessel, the dhow. Suakin (sometimes spelt Suakim) was active in the times of the Pharaohs of Ancient Egypt, and an old-established caravan track ran inland to reach the Nile at the town of Berber. From the earliest days of railway development in the Sudan, a line following this "Red Sea route" from Suakin to the Nile was always in the mind of the planners. This rail link, connecting to the national 3ft 6in. gauge system close to the Nile at Atbara, near Berber, was finally completed in 1905. However, Suakin was not to become the permanent coastal terminus of the Red Sea Railway as its harbour could not handle large commercial steamships.

A new "railway port" – Port Sudan – was developed some 36ml. to the north, with a branch line (soon to become the main line) from Sallom Junction on the route to Suakin. It was significant that when Lord Cromer officially inaugurated the Red Sea Railway on 27 January 1906, he did so at the site of the new Port Sudan, and not at the ancient port of Suakin. Was it also significant that the date chosen was almost precisely 21 years to the day since General Gordon had been killed at Khartoum on 26 January 1885? Lord Cromer, as Sir Evelyn Baring, had been the British Representative to the Egyptian Government in Cairo during the dramatic events of the 1880s in the Sudan, as discussed below. It was from Suakin and Port Sudan that equipment came by sea to Trinkitat to build and operate the two railways. In return, cotton from the Tokar area, transported on the TTLR, was shipped from Trinkitat to these larger ports for processing.

As well as the two railways from Trinkitat, three other small railway systems in the area will also be discussed, one of 18in. and two of 2ft gauge. These can be summarised as follows:

c) an 18in. gauge military supply system in the Suakin area, built by the British Royal Engineers in 1884/5 to support the ill-fated Suakin-Berber Railway project, and largely dismantled in 1885 when that project failed;

d) the Tokar Sand Clearance rail system, of 2ft gauge and using up to 7.5 miles of track, built and operated in 1937/38 on the eastern side of Tokar to allow the Sudan Public Works Department to reposition extensive sand deposits which were threatening the town;

e) a "narrow gauge" (probably 2ft gauge) internal transport system within the docks at Port Sudan, which was operating in the mid 1920s.

Material left behind from the system at Suakin was used to build the 18in. gauge military railway to El Teb. Locomotives and other equipment for the Tokar Sand Clearance, after delivery by sea to Trinkitat, were transported to Tokar over the TTLR.

The narrow gauge system at Port Sudan was reported by another formidable figure, Felix J. C. Pole, General Manager of the Great Western Railway, whose involvement in railways so far from Paddington will be explained later.

With lightly-built railways of a gauge close to two feet, the precise gauge to which track was laid and maintained, and to which wheels were set, is difficult to determine. As far as possible, "2ft gauge" is used here when describing these systems generally, but "600mm. gauge" is used when it was specifically noted in written sources. On the subject of measurement more generally, the units as used in sources, whether Imperial or metric, have been quoted unaltered and without conversion equivalents. It is relevant, however, to quote conversion factors for two Sudanese units, the kantar for weight and the feddan for land area and for nautical cable, as used in Admiralty publications on Trinkitat Harbour:

1 kantar = 99 lbs	1 ton = 22.6 kantar
1 feddan = 1.04 acres	1 acre = 0.96 feddan
1 cable = 0.1 nautical mile = 200 yards (approx.)	

Sudan and the Red Sea Coast

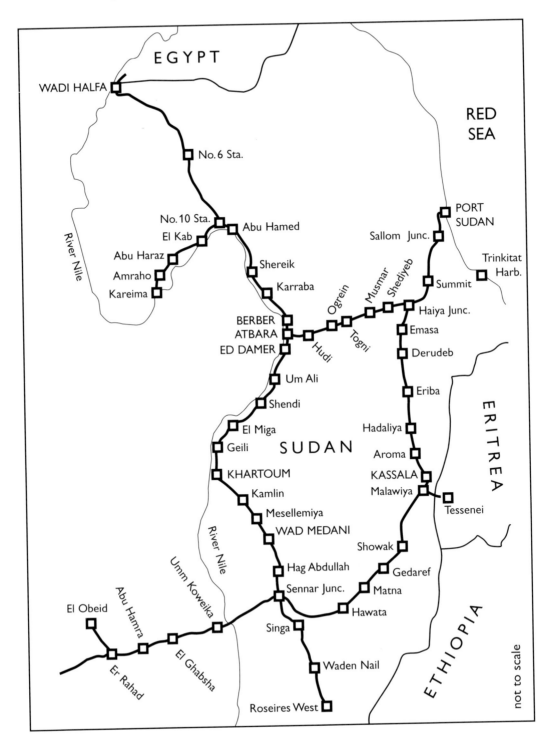

x

Chapter 1
SOME SUDANESE HISTORY

To set these small railways in context, some Sudanese history is necessary. From the 1820s, the political and commercial influence of Turkish-dominated Egypt spread southwards along the River Nile into the lands which now form the Sudan. An administrative capital was set up by the Nile at Khartoum. In 1865, Suakin and its surrounding area was ceded by the government of Turkey to Egypt. Soon afterwards, according to Hill, "a dynamic, if eccentric, governor", Ahmad Mumtaz Pasha, laid the foundation of cotton cultivation in the delta of the Khor Baraka by establishing a plantation at Tokar. We have already noted the initial plans at this time for building a railway between Tokar and Trinkitat to handle the cotton crop.

Following the opening of the Suez Canal in 1869, Britain became deeply involved in Egyptian affairs, and a number of Britons took senior positions in the Egyptian army and civil administration. However, Egyptian rule was not popular in the Sudan. In the early 1880s Mohammed Ahmed Ibn el-Sayyid Abdullah, a charismatic leader soon to become known as the Mahdi, launched a jihad (an Islamic Holy War) against foreigners. By 1883 fighting had spread to the Red Sea coast around Suakin and Tokar, the local Sudanese leader being Osman Digna. In November 1883 the Mahdi's followers totally overwhelmed an Egyptian force of over 7000, led by a British Colonel, William Hicks, south-west of Khartoum.

According to Anthony Nutting in his book "Gordon, martyr and misfit" the Hicks disaster was a turning point in British involvement in the Sudan. Prime Minister Gladstone – already committed to the withdrawal of the British from Egypt – had no wish whatever to become involved with the crisis in the Sudan. But Britain was already too deeply enmeshed in Egyptian affairs "and henceforth … found herself committed," continued Nutting, "not only to running and reforming Egypt and recreating her Army, but still more to directing the policy of evacuating the Sudan. Gladstone's Cabinet had drifted into the very position which they had sought so strenuously to avoid." Faced with these circumstances, Nutting noted, "their thoughts turned inevitably to Charles Gordon … the only man with the necessary experience and reputation to extricate them from these unwelcome responsibilities." General Gordon was one of the most famous (and complex) personalities of the era of British imperial expansion. He had already served as "Governor General of the Sudan and the Red Sea Littoral" for the Egyptian Government, but had left Khartoum in 1879. He was thought to have unique powers to negotiate with the Mahdi, and to organise the safe evacuation of Egyptian officials and soldiers from the Sudan.

In January 1884, on a wave of British public Jingoism, Gordon left Charing Cross Station in London to become, once again, Governor General of the Sudan. Whilst Sir

Evelyn Baring pursued all possible diplomatic avenues in Cairo, Gordon went up the Nile. Following an increasingly traumatic existence in Khartoum, all Gordon's bids for peace failed. Finally on 26 January 1885 – a key date in Sudanese history – Gordon met his death on the steps of the Governor General's Palace. Whilst the Mahdi's followers celebrated, Victorian Britain – from the Queen downwards – was devasted by this blow to Imperial arrogance and complacency. A highly idealised painting of Gordon's death became almost an icon in contemporary culture. The Mahdi died soon after, but his followers continued to control much of the Sudan until the Battle of Omdurman in 1898. In this epic confrontation, across the Nile from Khartoum, massed Sudanese forces were defeated by British and Egyptians led by General Kitchener.

In the following year, 1899, the "Anglo-Egyptian Condominium" was set up to manage Sudanese affairs, and British influence steadily expanded after the First World War. Following an increasing role of Sudanese people in government and professional life, the Sudan became an independent country in 1955, shortly after the Tokar-Trinkitat Light Railway – the last survivor of the five small narrow gauge railways discussed here – was dismantled.

For simplicity, the name "Sudan Railways" (SR) has been used throughout the book to indicate the national 3ft 6in. railway system, although it was only officially adopted as a title in 1932. Hill supplied the following more historical titles:

1896 – 1902 Sudan Military Railway
1902 – 1918 Sudan Government Railways
1918 – 1930 Sudan Government Railways and Steamers
1930 – 1932 Sudan Government Railways

Chapter 2

THE 18-INCH GAUGE MILITARY RAILWAYS AT SUAKIN, 1884/85

When General Gordon met his death in January 1885, plans were almost complete at Suakin to launch what was to be one of the greatest disasters in British military railway construction, the Suakin-Berber Railway. "From every point of view except perhaps the humorist's", wrote Hill, "the Suakin-Berber Railway was a failure. It was never completed; it was scarcely even begun. It carried no passengers and no profitable merchandise. It cost the British taxpayers close on a million pounds sterling." Just under a year earlier, in February 1884, Gordon had arrived in Khartoum. His mission, as quoted by Nutting, was "to arrange for the evacuation ... and safe removal of the Egyptian employees and troops" from the Sudan. As the year advanced, however, the situation in Khartoum, besieged by the Mahdi's forces, steadily deteriorated. To help break the Mahdi's hold on central Sudan, the British War Office planned a rail link along the "Red Sea route" between Suakin and Berber. It was decided to improve both the defences of Suakin, and its capacity as a port to land equipment for the Suakin-Berber Railway, which was to be built to the standard (European) gauge of 4ft 8^1/$_2$in.

In pursuit of these plans, Hill noted, the 17th Company, Royal Engineers was sent to Suakin in June 1884 to build jetties and lay down local light railways of 18in. gauge in order to prepare the port as a railway depot. By the summer of 1884, 18in. gauge lines ran between the waterfront and a chain of forts, together with a headquarters camp, outside the town. A shore base for both gauges was on Quarantine Island, north of the main town and dhow port. Nearby were banks of condensers, which produced fresh water from salt water, and a major role for the 18in. gauge was to transport the fresh water produced. The 18in. gauge trains were handled by VULCAN and MERCURY, 10 ton 0-4-2 tanks built by the Vulcan Foundry in 1883 and 1884 respectively. The use of light railways by the Royal Engineers is well covered in "An illustrated history of 18 inch gauge steam railways" by Mark Smithers. He noted that VULCAN and MERCURY had been built for use on the Fortifications railway at the School of Military Engineering at Chatham, where the technology of "trench railways" was developed.

The performance of the 18in. gauge railways at Suakin was the subject of a lively correspondence in "The Royal Engineers Journal" during 1885. In the July issue Captain H. G. Kunhardt argued that the metre gauge (as used in India) would have been best for the main Suakin-Berber Railway. Turning to what he mistakenly described as the 1ft 8in. gauge, Kunhardt wrote "The engines ... are only capable of hauling 25 tons at a speed of eight miles an hour, and are therefore not worth considering. They may be useful in arsenals and dockyards, or for connecting Engineer parks with the trenches during the siege of a large fortress, but for such purposes as supplying an army in the field with men, ammunition and stores at a distance of over five miles from the base, they are totally unsuitable. At Suakin, a 1ft 8in. engine and train, working day and night, was only just able to supply the headquarter camp and two regiments with water at a distance of 1.5ml. from the base."

A spirited response came in the August issue from Captain W. W. Robinson at Chatham, who felt impelled "to write a line in defence of the 1ft 6in. gauge, as a sort of tribute of affection to my two little friends, the VULCAN and MERCURY locomotives which had done us such good service on the Chatham forts, and which I saw off for Suakin with feelings of regret, mingled with hope that they would do good service there." His spirited defence of VULCAN and MERCURY was based firstly on their very effective behaviour at the Chatham Fortifications. "However, not to quote the work on one particular line only, one day last week at Woolwich Arsenal the railway plant returned from Suakin was being unloaded and in the course of a day 237 tons of rails were loaded at the pier on to 95 trucks (the average load per truck being 2.5 tons, and about one-third of the trucks left empty to allow for overlap of 30ft rails); these were dragged by a single 1ft 6in. locomotive to the depot on Plumstead marshes, 2.5ml. distant. And, again, 223 tons (net load) were similarly transported the next day." Robinson did concede, however, that 2ft 6in. gauge, then under serious military consideration, might have advantages of scale over the 18in. gauge. By July 1885, when he wrote this letter, the life of the Suakin-Berber Railway was already over, as we shall see.

"Had Captain Robinson seen his 'little friends' at Suakin he would probably not have recognised them." responded Kunhardt in a letter in the December issue. This had been written on September 5, 1885 at "Camp, Barak Pass, Baluchistan" on the Indian North-West Frontier. "They could be heard a mile off, very consumptive, with their bones all rattling. I have not the slightest doubt that the engines at Woolwich and Chatham can easily do what Captain Robinson says they do. A sound horse can drag far more over a planked road than a lame one over a ploughed field; and it is the lame horse and the ploughed field that have to be dealt with in a military railway on service." The driver of a water train at Suakin had told Kunhardt that whilst VULCAN and MERCURY could run at a reasonable speed with two wagons carrying between them four 500 gallon tanks (around 10 tons net load), they only ran very slowly with three wagons carrying six water tanks. After noting that the closeness of small 18in. gauge engines to the ground made them prone to getting dust and grit in their bearings, Kunhardt returned to his championship of Indian metre gauge practice for military lines. "With a war in Egypt or in Persia, in South Africa, Burmah, or China, or even in the Black Sea, would it be advisable to first make and then send out a 2ft 6in. gauge railway from England, in preference to at once dispatching a metre gauge line from Bombay?"

Whether or not 2ft 6in. or metre gauges had been considered, there had been major disagreements over the gauge of the main Suakin-Berber Railway, whose construction the 18in. gauge military lines were to support. Williams noted that "18in. was championed, 3ft 6in. decided upon, and ... 4ft 8^1/$_2$ in. material actually sent [from Britain], along with 75 navvies, complete with corduroy trousers and bowler hats, to lay the track." Hill noted that in fact 750 British navvies arrived at Suakin, in the employ of contractors Lucas and Aird, who were to build the line. Standard gauge Manning Wardle saddle tanks also arrived. The farcical story of the rise and fall of the Suakin-Berber Railway was well told in Hill's "Sudan Transport". Shipment of equipment from Britain started in February 1885, spurred on by the news of the death of General Gordon. During March, however, the very limited port facilities at Suakin also had to cope with the arrival of the 13,000-strong Suakin Field Force, which was to protect the construction of the line. By May only 19 miles of 4ft 8^1/$_2$ in. gauge track had been laid from Suakin to Otao, progress being limited partly by spirited opposition from Osman Digna's forces, but mainly by operational incompetence. Then the War Office changed its mind! Work was stopped, and the order was given to return equipment to England.

The magazine "Punch" summed up the whole Suakin-Berber Railway affair in a marvellous spoof timetable, reproduced in Hill's "Sudan Transport". This sported Bradshaw-style footnotes such as "B Stops by artillery fire only" and "D First and Second class passengers, not wishing to be sent across Central Africa in gangs and sold a bargain [as slaves] at Mtempsa, are advised to alight at the previous station and hide in the Mimosa bushes, and, if they can, catch the 9.17 Up train to Suakim."

So sudden was the War Office decision that twelve 18in. gauge 0-4-2 tanks, ordered from Fowler and Bagnall for use on the support lines at Suakin, had to be given other duties once delivered to the Royal Arsenal, Woolwich. In his article "The First Hundred Bagnalls" in "Industrial Railway Record" No. 100, Allan Baker quoted from "The Engineer" for 6 March 1885 (a report prepared in the confident early days of the Suakin-Berber Railway project): "Mr W. G. Bagnall, Castle Engine Works, Stafford, has obtained a considerable contract from Government for portable railway plant and small locomotives for the Sudan. This railway, it is understood, will be used as a feeder for the wider gauge permanent railway to be laid down by Messrs Lucas and Aird, conveying the materials for its construction and running alongside of it. As the order has to be completed within a limited time, it is intended to at once enlarge Mr Bagnall's works." Hill, however, reported political sleaze! "'Was it not a fact,' asked a querulous Member in the House of Commons, 'that the head of the Stafford firm which had received the contract for the locomotives was president of the Stafford Conservative Association?'" Bagnall's response to that comment is not recorded, but his problem with the War Office over the design of these locomotives is discussed below. Baker noted that Bagnall was, in fact Chairman – not President – of the Staffordshire Conservative Association, as well as being a County Councillor.

After the major military withdrawal in 1885, it must be assumed that sufficient rails, rolling stock and other equipment remained at Suakin for further use some ten years later to build the 18in. military line from Trinkitat to El Teb. Smithers concluded that VULCAN and MERCURY returned to Britain, and suggested in "The Narrow Gauge" No. 136 that some surplus 18in. gauge equipment, originally destined for Suakin, went to the Camden Fort military tramway near Cork in Ireland. A map of Suakin, published in the R E Journal for March 1886, appeared in Smithers' book. More details of VULCAN and MERCURY, of the Fowler and Bagnall locomotives ordered for work at Suakin and of wagon types appear in the section below on locomotives and rolling stock.

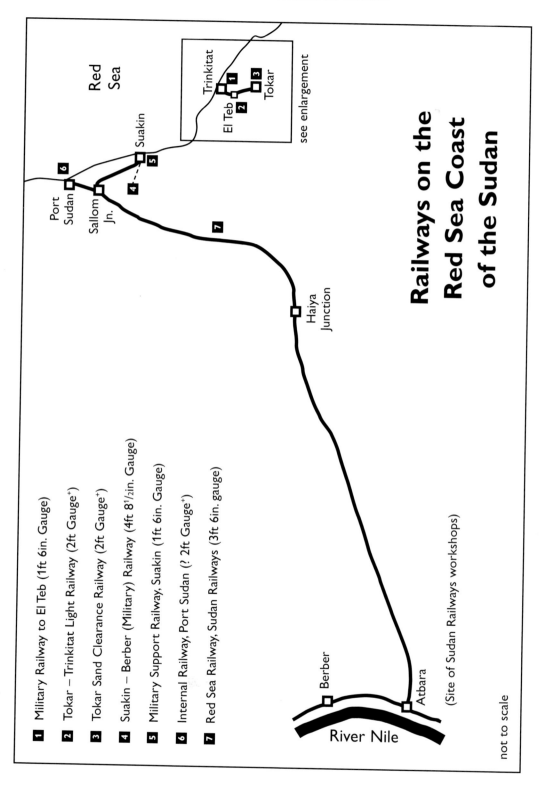

Railways on the
Red Sea Coast
of the Sudan

1 Military Railway to El Teb (1ft 6in. Gauge)

2 Tokar – Trinkitat Light Railway (2ft Gauge⁺)

3 Tokar Sand Clearance Railway (2ft Gauge⁺)

4 Suakin – Berber (Military) Railway (4ft 8½in. Gauge)

5 Military Support Railway, Suakin (1ft 6in. Gauge)

6 Internal Railway, Port Sudan (? 2ft Gauge⁺)

7 Red Sea Railway, Sudan Railways (3ft 6in. gauge)

(Site of Sudan Railways workshops)

not to scale

Chapter 3

THE 18-INCH GAUGE MILITARY RAILWAY TO THE WELLS AT EL TEB

After the excitements around Suakin in 1884/5, the 18in. gauge line from Trinkitat to El Teb was a quiet affair. Indeed, the precise purpose for which it was constructed is unclear. Its only recorded use was to transport water from the wells at El Teb to serve shipping at Trinkitat. When the line was laid down in 1896, however, the cotton crop was already established around Tokar. The proposal in 1871 for a railway to carry cotton to the coast has already been mentioned. Storrar confirmed that during the 1880s, despite the Mahdi's *jihad*, Egyptian Pashas (regional government officials) were keen to develop cotton growing around Tokar. Was this cotton crop the original reason behind the building of the 18in. gauge line?

General Kitchener was appointed Sirdar (commander) of the Egyptian Army in 1892, with a remit which included the Sudan. In a regional planning role (according to Hill) he proposed two railways in the Red Sea coastal area. One, predictably, was along the "Red Sea route" from Suakin to Berber, correcting the fiasco of 1885. The other route was to run south from Suakin, through Tokar and the rich cropping lands of the Khor Baraka delta to Kassala, an important town further south. "Whatever Kitchener's railway ambitions," continued Hill, "the funds at his disposal were small. All that eventuated from these splendid visions was a causeway, built by Lieutenant G. F. Gorringe from Trinkitat harbour to the mainland on which a railway of 18in. gauge and 40lb. rails was laid 10km. (7ml.) inland as far as El Teb where a small running shed was put up." An Admiralty chart of Trinkitat Harbour in the 1890s showed a single track ending at a short pier with no sidings.

In July 1896 two military surveyors, Captain Bower and Lieut-Colonel Count Gleichen, rode inland from Trinkitat, as reported in Gleichen's "The Anglo-Egyptian Sudan". "For 2.5ml. from Trinkitat the road runs along a broad embankment, on which for one mile an 18in. gauge railway has been laid down. After leaving the embankment there is a sandy stretch, and then about two miles of narrow embankment just broad enough for the railway line. This embankment in places has rather a serpentine course, and would have to be straightened before rails could be laid down. At El Teb there is a small fort, and an ample supply of water at a depth of 17ft." Walter Ellis suggested that a 1.5ml. causeway at Trinkitat was built before 1884 by prison labour under the direction of Governor Mumtaz Pasha, whose enthusiasm for the cotton crop was noted earlier.

When Bower and Gleichen reached El Teb on their military survey, they found the well water to be slightly brackish, although the men quartered at the small fort there "spoke well of it". The fort had a brick wall 10ft high and 18in. thick, a ditch 11ft broad and 8ft deep, and a signal tower 43ft high – matching one at Tokar. The area saw considerable fighting between Sudanese and Anglo-Egyptian forces in 1883/84. At the time of the Hicks disaster in late 1883, Osman Digna, the Mahdi's champion along the Red Sea coast, had besieged Egyptian garrisons in the area, including those at Suakin and Tokar. His determined supporters from the Hadendowa tribe were formidable fighting opponents, and Rudyard Kipling recorded a British soldier's respect for their valour in battle in one of his poems of British Army life overseas. Two Egyptian expeditions sent to relieve the besieged Tokar garrison were both badly defeated in the El Teb area, one in November 1883 and the other in January 1884.

Finally, a British force under General Sir Gerald Graham overcame the Sudanese forces at the "Battle of El Teb" on 29 February 1884 and then went on to relieve the garrison at Tokar. The events of this battle were recorded by another British poet, the Scottish bard of Dundee, William McGonagall. Although most famous (or infamous) for his poem "The Tay Bridge Disaster", McGonagall also burst into verse on a wide range of late Victorian battles and tragedies. His poetic coverage of the Sudanese military campaign was extensive; in addition to "The Battle of El Teb", other (largely forgettable) gems from his pen were "General Gordon, the Hero of Khartoum" and "The Battle of Omdurman".

Much of this fighting close to El Teb in the 1880s took place around what later became the terminus site of the 18in. gauge line, and gruesome skeletal relics lingered as track-side features into the days of the TTLR. From the tracklaying progress noted by Bower and Gleichen in July 1896, the 18in. gauge line must surely have been completed to El Teb during the same year. Hill suggested that the locomotives, wagons and track came from the light railways at Suakin, despite the peak of military activity there having been ten years earlier. However, the delivery date of the only locomotive to be associated with the line, a Bagnall 0-4-0 inverted saddle tank named RAMESES, is clearly listed as February 1896 in the Bagnall Locomotive Works List produced in 1984 by Baker and Allen Civil. Some confusion exists over the Bagnall consignment address for RAMESES. In their Oakwood Press book "Bagnalls of Stafford" (1973), Baker and Civil gave the destination as "E. Legget (War Office) Dp. Suakim Berber Railway, Egypt", which would indicate delivery in 1896 to whatever British (Royal Engineers) military base remained at Suakin. Gorringe would have then had to arrange transport to Trinkitat by sea. In the 1984 Bagnall Works List, however, the consignment address for RAMESES was changed to "E. Legget (War Office) Dp. Tokar Trinkitat Light Railway, Sudan." Whilst this implies delivery direct to Trinkitat, the title "Tokar Trinkitat Light Railway" correctly relates only to the later 600mm. gauge line. More recently, Baker has advised that one Bagnall register listed the customer as the Egyptian Government, and that the agent was E. H. M. Leggett.

RAMESES, the Bagnall 0-4-0 IST of the 18-inch gauge military line, during excavation at the site of the El Teb locomotive shed in 1921.

A possible source of confusion is that RAMESES survived into the early days of the TTLR. In 1921 G. R. Storrar, as the senior Sudan Railways civil engineer involved in planning the 600mm. gauge line, visited El Teb with the contractors who were to build the TTLR, Arthur Ellis and a Mr Vincent. Old 18in. gauge track ran close to the fort and there was also a siding and the remains of small engine shed. Near to the shed was an old locomotive, almost entirely buried in the sand. "Vincent and Ellis have now dug it out, and it looks a weird object in such an outlandish situation," wrote Storrar. From photographs this was clearly a Bagnall inverted saddle tank – by implication RAMESES. Hill may have unwittingly added to the confusion through a photograph in "Sudan Transport", which showed the 18in. gauge Bagnall after excavation. The caption states "Tokar-Trinkitat Light Railway: early locomotive at El-Teb", when RAMESES was not, of course, a 600mm. gauge TTLR locomotive.

No details have so far been discovered of the wagons used to carry water from El Teb to Trinkitat. Those mentioned by Kunhardt in use around Suakin carried two 500gl. water tanks each, and Smithers in his book illustrates designs of 18in. gauge bogie wagons, developed by the Royal Engineers in the late 19th century, which could have transported such tanks. These wagon designs, together with RAMESES, are covered in more detail in the section below on locomotives and rolling stock. The weight of rail

What appears to be excavated 18-inch gauge track from the military railway. Piles of steel sleepers stand around, presumably awaiting the laying of track for the TTLR along the same alignment.

quoted by Hill (40lb.) is of interest. Smithers noted that the RE "Manual of Military Railways" for 1889 proposed 24lb. as a suitable weight for 18in. gauge military railways. However, during a visit to Woolwich Arsenal in the 1890s, Leslie S. Robertson noted that 41.25lb. flat bottom rail using an Indian State Railways section was in use there, as reported in an Appendix to his paper "Narrow gauge railways – two feet and under". Smithers also noted that 41lb. rail was standard for the 18in. gauge lines at Woolwich.

Little else seems to have been recorded on the 18in. gauge military railway. Hill noted that by 1904 the line had fallen into disrepair, although camel-drawn trains were still carrying water from El Teb wells to supply shipping at Trinkitat. Some 18in. gauge track was still in position in 1921, and it seems likely that rails would have been used again for constructing the TTLR. The mystery remains as to why the 18in. gauge line was only built to El Teb. Kitchener had recognised the need for rail transport through the Tokar cotton growing area, and the Royal Engineers regarded the railway as a serious enough project to have ordered RAMESES. Trinkitat was never a large port, and although the water brought by rail from El Teb was no doubt welcomed by dhow captains and other mariners, the building of a remote railway with only one locomotive just for that traffic hardly makes sense. Admirality publications, discussed below in connection with port development at Trinkitat, did indicate in passing that this 18in. gauge line was completed to Tokar, but there is no other evidence to support that information. Did Gorringe, as Hill implies, simply run out of "project funding" once El Teb had been reached?

Chapter 4

COTTON, CAMELS, SAMBUKS...
AND SIR FELIX J. C. POLE

The purpose of the 600mm. gauge Tokar-Trinkitat Light Railway was primarily to carry the Tokar district cotton crop to Trinkitat for onward shipment. Before describing the line, it is therefore worth taking a brief look at how the cotton around Tokar was grown and processed, and how the crop was transported before the TTLR was built. The Khor Baraka is a seasonal river channel. Rains falling over its catchment upstream of Tokar normally cause flooding each year between mid July to late August. These flood waters spread across alluvial soils of the delta around Tokar and provide good conditions for the cultivation of cotton. Sharp and Williams described the cotton growing. Seed was issued by the Government, and planting took place during August and September. Amounts of rainfall on the Khor Baraka catchment varied from year to year, but usually about 100,000 acres would be flooded for cultivation, although food crops were needed as well as cotton. The boll (seed pod) of the cotton plant contains seeds with fibrous hairs attached. As it ripens it bursts open, clearly displaying the white fibres. Picked for harvest in this state, it is known as seed cotton. Cotton picking could start as early as February of the following year, depending on weather conditions. As the picking season progressed, however, weather conditions deteriorated. "During the months of June and July, i.e. prior to the Baraka flood," wrote Count Gleichen in 1905, "blinding dust storms prevail daily from 9 in the morning till 4 or 5 in the afternoon, and it is impossible to see more than a few yards in front of one ... In the summer of 1891, a party of cavalry were caught in one of these storms and had terrible experiences, losing many men and horses." The effect of sandstorms on railway operation is discussed below.

The transport of the annual seed cotton harvest to Trinkitat was a major logistic exercise. Williams wrote that before the advent of the TTLR, 1500 camels were needed to transport the cotton crop to Trinkitat "... the sight of a camel with a huge sack containing 350-400 pounds of seed cotton tied on both sides of him was one to remember." By 1921, according to Storrar, up to 500 camels per day unloaded bales on the small jetties at Trinkitat at the peak of the transport season. That must have provided not only sights, but also sounds and smells, to remember!

From Trinkitat the seed cotton was originally shipped to Suakin by the variety of Arab dhow known as the *sambuk*. John Jewell in his book "Dhows at Mombasa" describes a typical sambuk as varying in displacement from 75 to 140 tons, with average length and beam of 80ft and 20ft. In TTLR days, according to Sharp and Williams,

Across the seed cotton bales at Trinkitat. TTLR tracks run between the bales, and a collection of sambuk await loading.

the crop was also transported from Trinkitat to Suakin and Port Sudan by two small steamers SS TOKAR and TALODI. The TALODI gained fame in the Sudan Railways Annual Report for 1929, having damaged the main quay at Port Sudan whilst berthing on 8 July. She was noted as a ship of 743 tons, owned by the Khedivial Mail Steamship Co., details which probably also applied to her sister ship TOKAR. An Ellis photograph showed a similar small steamer named SUDANI. In later years (according to Sharp and Williams) seed cotton bales were loaded onto Sudan Railways pontoons (or lighters), which were towed by tugs from Trinkitat to Port Sudan.

Seed cotton has to be subjected to a process known as ginning to separate the fibre (lint) from the seeds, and the ginneries (ginning factories) which processed the Tokar crop were sited at Suakin and Port Sudan. The operation of a typical African ginnery is described in a 1935 handbook on Uganda by H. B. Thomas and Robert Scott "The seed cotton enters the ginnery by way of the opener room in which the cotton, which has probably arrived in a packed condition containing some dirt, is passed through a seed cotton opener which teases out the lint on the seed and by means of a fan eliminates a considerable proportion of the leaf and dirt... The seed cotton is then fed evenly into the roller gins [typically Platt's double-acting] ... The action of the roller gin is one of a pulling action in which the lint is dragged off the seed. This is effected by means of two knives, one fixed and pressing tightly against a roller, the other moving up and down behind the fixed knife. The rollers consist of either buffalo hide or fibre disks mounted on a central shaft, and revolve away from a fixed knife. The lint fibres adhere to the roller, and the moving knife detaches the seed from the lint. The seed falls through a grid and is delivered down chutes to the lower storey of the ginnery. The lint is then collected and carried along to the press box [typically John Shaw's hydraulic], where it is baled for shipment to a density of 25 lb. a cubic foot." The bales of compressed cotton produced weighed around 500 lb.

At this point the unlikely figure of Felix J. C. Pole, General Manager of the Great Western Railway, enters our story. In 1924 he reported, by invitation, on the operations of the Sudan Railways. In 1931, after having been knighted, he reported again. Pole made inspection visits to the Sudan, although there are no reports of the Great Man from Paddington actually visiting Tokar or Trinkitat. His 1924 Report mentioned a railway-owned ginnery which had operated at Port Sudan since 1918. According to the SR's own Annual Report for 1924, this plant was at that time handling cotton from Tokar, as well as from Berber and Dongola Provinces. Pole's 1931 Report noted that a new ginnery was being built at Port Sudan (not to be railway operated). There was an old ginnery at Suakin, which was the major source of employment there. Williams described it as "of antiquarian interest". Also of antiquarian interest were the remains near El Teb of an unsuccessful attempt to establish a ginnery in the Tokar area. These relics, seen by Storrar in 1921 and later by Walter Ellis in the 1930s, comprised parts of an ancient beam engine, plus a Lancashire boiler. They will be described below.

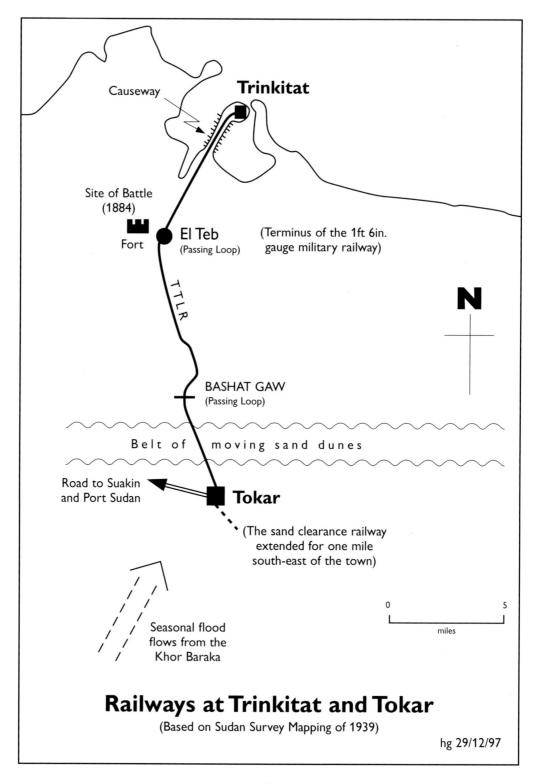

Causeway

Trinkitat

Site of Battle
(1884)

Fort

El Teb
(Passing Loop)

(Terminus of the 1ft 6in.
gauge military railway)

TTLR

N

BASHAT GAW
(Passing Loop)

Belt of moving sand dunes

Road to Suakin
and Port Sudan

Tokar

(The sand clearance railway
extended for one mile
south-east of the town)

Seasonal flood
flows from the
Khor Baraka

0   5
miles

Railways at Trinkitat and Tokar
(Based on Sudan Survey Mapping of 1939)

hg 29/12/97

Chapter 5

THE TOKAR-TRINKITAT LIGHT RAILWAY

Origins and questions of gauge

Although the 18in. gauge line to El Teb of 1896 does not seem to have transported seed cotton from the Tokar area, Hill noted that in 1910 a group of merchants from Alexandria applied to the Sudan Government to build a light railway from Trinkitat to Tokar, but negotiations broke down. There were various plans to build a 3ft 6in. gauge branch line to transport the cotton crop from Tokar by rail, leaving the main SR system shortly west of Suakin. These proposals are discussed below under "Alternative Links from Tokar to the Red Sea Coast". However, as Hill recorded, "Early in 1921 plans were made to restore Kitchener's light railway [the 1896 line to El Teb] and prolong it to Tokar. This was not then regarded as an end in itself but only as a temporary expedient until the 3ft 6in. Suakin-Tokar line could be completed." Following the "temporary expedient" thinking, the TTLR was built and operated not by Sudan Railways, but by two contractors, Messrs Vincent and (Arthur) Ellis. When Storrar, as the senior SR civil engineer involved in the project, visited the Tokar and Trinkitat areas in February 1921, he had extended discussions with Vincent and Ellis, and also met local officials of the Government Agriculture Department, which supervised cotton growing in the Tokar district. Together with Vincent and Ellis, he searched for a station site near the cotton market in Tokar. Moving to Trinkitat, Storrar found three small jetties which he felt to be totally inadequate for the enormous amount of cotton which needed transporting. His estimate was 12,000 tons in a good year. Water supply was a significant problem, and continued to be so on the TTLR. Eventually tanks were erected at Trinkitat, supplied with water by Sudan Railways tugs from Port Sudan.

Whilst Storrar returned to SR Headquarters at Atbara in mid-February 1921 to complete his report on the TTLR project, Arthur Ellis, Vincent and their men continued work. Sharp noted that the first rail was laid on 20 February 1921 and that the line was opened to traffic in March of the following year, 1922. All materials were brought in to Trinkitat by sea, including 18 and 20 lb. rail. Sharp recorded the line as being built to 2ft gauge. Walter Ellis, however, was clear that the original gauge was 600mm. He spoke from direct experience of the arrival of two new diesel locomotives from Hawthorn Leslie of Newcastle-upon-Tyne at Trinkitat in 1933. "As they [Hawthorn Leslie] did not cooperate with us they made some vital errors" Walter noted. On wheel gauge, he concluded that as gauge of the main Sudan Railways system

Early days on the TTLR, 1921/22. An Orenstein & Koppel 0-4-0 tank at the head of a train of tracklaying material. The wagons appear to be "C" class, those at the front carrying steel sleepers.

was of "Imperial" dimensions (3ft 6in.), Hawthorn Leslie assumed that the TTLR was of the "Imperial" 2ft gauge, "quite wrong it was metric (60 cm.). Two feet equals 61 centimetres ... this meant on the sharp curves of a small gauge railway the flanges on the wheels would **bind** on **every** curve on **all** wheels **each side,** a strain for the loco and bad for wheels ... So we had to alter the track on every curve or points."

By comparison, it is worth recording Hill's comments on the steam tramways in Khartoum, which, like the TTLR, started operations with small Orenstein & Koppel tank locomotives. The first Khartoum steam tramway line was inaugurated in 1904, having been laid to 2ft gauge. "Its locomotives and rolling stock were of 600mm. gauge, a disparity with the gauge of the track which caused the earliest tramcars to lurch dramatically while negotiating curves. Later the gauge of the track was altered to the gauge of the wheels running on it." Precisely the reverse situation to that experienced by Walter Ellis. A difficulty with these 600mm./2ft gauge discussions is clarifying when "two feet" meant precisely 24in. and when it was used as shorthand for 1ft 11⅝in. – the exact "Imperial" equivalent of 600mm. Was the problem with the TTLR Hawthorn Leslies also related to wheelbase and wheel profiles?

Operation by contractors, 1922 to 1932/33

The Tokar-Trinkitat Light Railway had two broad periods of life. From 1922 to around 1932 it was managed and operated by the contractors, firstly Vincent and Ellis, and later Arthur Ellis alone. From 1933, although Arthur and Walter Ellis seem to have still been involved, it came more fully under Sudan Railways control until closure in

Two TTLR Simplexes, WDLR 2234 and 2190, with trains of equipment, probably in the early 1920s. The rear end sheets of the Simplexes have been removed. The train behind 2234 appears to be of "C" class wagons, and the "D" class wagons behind 2190 have not yet been fitted with end stanchions to retain cotton bales.

1952. Hill recorded that the TTLR started operation with five 30hp. 0-4-0 steam locomotives built by Orenstein & Koppel of Berlin and 36 assorted wagons. These were brought from Port Sudan to Trinkitat on Sudan Railways tugs. From an Ellis photograph, the O & K locomotives appear to have been standard "off-the-peg" contractors well tanks. They do not seem to have been used for long, probably due to the severe water supply problems noted by Storrar, and Hill recorded that three were scrapped in 1922. Four ex-War Department Light Railways (WDLR) 40hp. Simplex internal combustion locomotives took their place. The O & K and Simplex locomotives came second hand to the TTLR. Their possible origins and technical details are discussed below in the section on locomotives.

The wagons with which the TTLR started operations were also "War Surplus". What seem to be the very simple WDLR "C" class bogie wagons appear in photographs of construction days. However, the majority were of the WDLR "D" class bogie design, fine illustrated coverage of which appeared in "The Ashover Light Railway" by Robert Gratton and Stuart Band. They describe the "D" class wagons as "... having been constructed in two varieties, one with wooden underframes and the other with steel. Both had timber bodies comprising fixed ends and drop-down sides with a removable centre post which allowed the side doors to be dropped down either individually or together." These wagons had flat floors, with internal dimensions 17ft 8^1/$_2$in. long and 4ft 9^1/$_2$in. wide. To carry seed cotton bales, Arthur Ellis had two upright steel stanchions fixed at each end of the wagons. Attached to the tops of these stanchions were steel rings through which ropes were passed to hold the bales steady. This allowed 24 bales to be carried, eight crosswise along on the floor, with two layers of eight above them. Photographs also showed wagons of what appear to be the closely-related WDLR "F" class design. These had sunken storage wells between the bogies, in which extra bales could carried. Like the "D" class, they had steel stanchions attached at each end for retaining cotton bales. David Ellis noted that, as the line had no steep gradients, Arthur removed the brake gear from the bogies of most WDLR wagons, thus eliminating lodging sites for unwanted and abrasive sand. More information on TTLR wagons appears in the later section on rolling stock.

According to Walter Ellis and Sharp, the 40hp. Simplexes were capable of hauling trains of eight bogie wagons, carrying 192 seed cotton bales. Walter noted that it was common practice for one Simplex to haul two eight-wagon trains back to Tokar, as the volume of incoming traffic was not large. However, Sharp wrote that in later years a good deal of traffic for merchants in Tokar was brought in by sea to Trinkitat for onward transit via the TTLR. It is unclear on what scale "official" passenger traffic operated. Ellis and Williams photographs show travellers perched on top of wagon

TTLR Simplex WDLR 2126 with a passenger "coach" created from a "D" class wagon. The right hand end sheet of the Simplex has been removed. As the chimney of RAMESES appears behind the cab, the view must date from 1921/22.

Sand clearance on the TTLR – an annual challenge. A Hawthorn Leslie stands on the "main line" with a collection of "D" class wagons, including two carrying water tanks. All are fitted with end stanchions for carrying cotton bales. The V-skips appear to be on a separate line laid to help clear the sand, which was loaded by men using woven baskets of the type stacked on the nearest wagon.

A group takes a break at Trinkitat by the earlier inspection railcar "TTLR No. 1", which appears to be a Drewry/Baguley product. Arthur Ellis, sporting his cummerbund, stands on the left, with one of the small steamers at the main jetty behind him.

loads of cotton bales, but it is not clear if they actually had to pay for these precarious perches. In TTLR accounts contained in Sudan Railways Annual Reports during the 1920s, small receipt figures appear for "passengers". Arthur Ellis had some tickets printed, and one of the WDLR "D" class wagons was converted into a makeshift passenger coach. The planked sides were cut away at one end on each side, allowing passenger access, and benches provided seating. The sun was kept at bay by a roof and side awnings. For transporting senior management the TTLR had motor inspection railcars, the first of which appears from photographs to have been a Drewry/Baguley product.

Running the TTLR was not easy. "The operating difficulties" wrote Hill "were prodigious. The contractors ran trains during six months of the year and during the remaining six months dug the track out of the sand drifts, maintained the railway, and recovered elsewhere from the heat, which is probably the most trying in all the Sudan." Sharp confirmed that the line was closed annually during the summer, when the sandstorms occurred. The 1932 edition of the Admiralty navigation guide the "Red Sea Pilot" noted: "A railway runs from the store near the pier [at Trinkitat] to El Teb and Tokar; but as during June, July and August, the weather is intensely hot and strong northerly winds and heavy dust storms are experienced, Tokar is then to a large extent evacuated, and the railway cannot be relied upon." Williams experienced the heat and sandstorms at first hand. "My first visit to Tokar was late in the [cotton-cropping] season, during a dense sandstorm when I found the Manager of the Tokar-Trinkitat Light Railway [Arthur Ellis?] having a novel lunch. His place was laid in the drawer of the dining table. He would open the draw, take a fork-full of food, and close the drawer again, it was his standard procedure for that time in the season."

Arthur Ellis, famous locally for the distinctive cummerbund he wore round his waist, was a man with a variety of engineering interests. During Walter's time with the TTLR in the 1930s, according to David Ellis, Arthur was quite frequently away supervising other engineering works. His business card of this period reads:

Phone Nos   Established 1920
93 Port Sudan 4 Tokar

A. W. ELLIS
ENGINEER & CONTRACTOR

Port Sudan & Tokar (Sudan)   Famagusta (Cyprus)
CONTRACTOR FOR SUPPLY AND ERECTION OF STRUCTURAL
STEELWORK, EITHER LIGHT OR HEAVY.

Workshops at Port Sudan and Tokar for General Repairs to Diesel, Petrol and
Paraffin Motors, Tractors, Motor Cars and Light Locomotives.

Repairs executed to Windmills, Pumps and any kind of Machinery.

Oxypet Cutting and Welding appliances available.

Heavy Tackle & Lifting Appliances on Hire up to 50 tons capacity.

One interesting project in Tokar which Arthur Ellis supervised was the construction of a fine mosque by local craftsmen. The TTLR was specially extended to allow the delivery of materials to the mosque site. The reasons for the transfer of management of the TTLR from Arthur Ellis to Sudan Railways in 1932/33 have not yet come to light. It may have been that Arthur's expanding business elsewhere, including significant work at Port Sudan, led him to decide to relinquish control.

Under Sudan Railways control, 1932/33 to 1952

In 1932 (according to Hill) the track was relaid, chiefly with 42lb. rails recovered from the long-abandoned SR Wadi Halfa-Kerma Railway. By 1945, Sharp reported, the original rails had been entirely replaced by 50lb. rails, again provided second-hand

Building the mosque at Tokar. TTLR Simplex WDLR 2143 heads a short train comprising a "D" class wagon which was converted to form a passenger vehicle and a second "D" class, with one half-side dropped for unloading what look like bags of cement. Although 2143 appears as an "open" type WDLR Simplex (with its rear end sheet removed), a view in "Railways and war before 1918" by Bishop and Davis, shows the same number carried by a fully enclosed "armoured" type.

from elsewhere on the SR system. David Ellis noted that steel sleepers were used inland, where wooden sleepers were at risk from termites, and wooden sleepers nearer to the sea, where salt corrosion of steel sleepers was likely. Sharp confirmed that wood sleepers were laid in the salt lake area which extended some 6ml. inland from Trinkitat. He added that standard SR 3ft 6in. steel sleepers (designed for 50 lb. rail) were drilled at Tokar to suit the 2ft gauge, and fitted with clips made in workshop there. Rails were spiked down directly on the wooden sleepers. By the workshops at Tokar, Arthur and Walter Ellis operated a "rail straightening machine shop".

Also in 1932, two 90hp. 0-4-0 diesel locomotives were ordered from R. & W. Hawthorn Leslie of Forth Banks Works, Newcastle-upon-Tyne. Walter Ellis explained that Sudan Railways wished to try out diesels before ordering large, expensive locomotives for the 3ft 6in. gauge main line. These two HLs for the TTLR were therefore the first diesels to run on the SR. "If they were OK on the dirt-ridden TTLR," Walter noted, "they should be OK for main line." He found design faults, some of which were later corrected, and design modifications he proposed were incorporated into a third similar locomotive, ordered in 1934. Despite the teething troubles, Hill noted that the SR General Manager was so impressed by the "mechanical efficiency" of the TTLR Hawthorn Leslies that he forecast, correctly, that diesel traction would also be successful on the main 3ft 6in. gauge system. Details of the three

Hawthorn Leslie SR 56 heads a train of seed cotton bales across typical salt-flat scrub country. The original cab has been modified to Walter Ellis' requirements, and the first vehicle is the special brake wagon, adapted from a "D" class. The driver's assistant operated the hand brake wheel on the pillar on the front bogie. The vertical stanchions were inset from the ends, reducing the bale load to eighteen. The next five wagons have centre wells, so were almost certainly "F" class.

The Wickham motor inspection railcar plus a trailer, which seems to be fitted with a tool box/bench seat. Probably on arrival (sometime in the 1930s?) as the paint looks shiny, and the railcar seats appear to be still wrapped for transit. The crest below the front light may be that of Sudan Railways. Almost certainly a replacement for the earlier Drewry/Baguley railcar.

HLs, together with Walter's pithy comments on the shortcomings of the original design, appear in the section on locomotives.

These diesels normally hauled 24 wagons fully loaded, according to Walter and Sharp, carrying 570-580 bales of seed cotton. Walter felt that they could have pulled more wagons, but sharp curves at stations and sand moving about by strong winds, often covering the track, made longer trains inadvisable. As Arthur had removed the brakes from most wagons, a special braking wagon was prepared for use on these longer trains, based on a "D" class. The original brakes were restored, operated by a hand wheel on a pillar mounted on each bogie. The cotton bale stanchions were inset from the wagon ends to allow clearance for the brake wheels to be turned. This meant that the braking wagon carried three tiers of six bales, 18 as opposed to 24 on a normal "D" class. Walter noted that this wagon was always placed right behind the locomotive and could be operated by the engine driver's assistant. Running from Tokar to Trinkitat (with a full load) the extra brake could be reached directly from the driver's cab. On the return journey the assistant needed to go round onto the front footplate to operate the wagon brake. However, as return trains were mostly empty, the locomotive brakes alone were usually sufficient. There was apparently only one wagon of this type. A Wickham inspection railcar, complete with four-wheeled trailer, was introduced, no doubt replacing the earlier Drewry/Baguley one.

It has not yet proved possible to check each Sudan Railways Annual Report over the period of life of the TTLR for financial and other details of the line's operation. Three Reports, for 1924, 1929 and 1932, reached the Public Record Office via GWR and British Transport Archives, having been provided to assist Felix J. C. Pole with his two surveys of Sudan Railways. The only mention of the TTLR in these Reports was in the financial appendices, under the heading "in accordance with the Agreement with Messrs Vincent and Ellis". By 1929 the Agreement is only with "Mr A. W. Ellis"; David Ellis thought that Mr Vincent may have had to leave the partnership due to ill health. Vincent and Ellis were paid an administration fee which, together with running expenses, had to be set against income. Sudan Railways also had to cover depreciation and interest charges. Taking those into account, the TTLR seems to have made an overall loss for the SR during the 1920s. However, cotton freight rates may well have been deliberately set at less than required to cover the full commercial costs, to assist the social and agricultural development of the Tokar district. Government subsidy for lines laid to develop agricultural traffic was by no means unknown amongst African railways. In addition, the annual cost of sand clearance from the track must have been significant. A later entry, in the SR Annual Report for 1937, speaks well of the profit that year, during which a record cotton crop was produced around Tokar. When Sharp was writing in 1945 an even better crop was forecast, with a total area under cotton of some 54,500 feddan (52,320 acres). He estimated that the crop would amount to 450,000 kantar (19,911 tons), despite a locust attack earlier in the season.

After this record traffic in 1945, however, the TTLR only survived for another seven years. According to Hill, competition by camel and lorry so reduced the available traffic that "the little undertaking was run at a financial loss". The end came in 1952, when the locomotives, rolling stock and track were transferred for use on the Gezira Light Railway. After all the trials of operating the Tokar-Trinkitat Light Railway, it was appropriate that two of its Hawthorn Leslie diesels, then some 20 years old, continued to work for the Sudan Gezira Board on the most extensive and successful 2ft gauge cotton-carrying railway in the world.

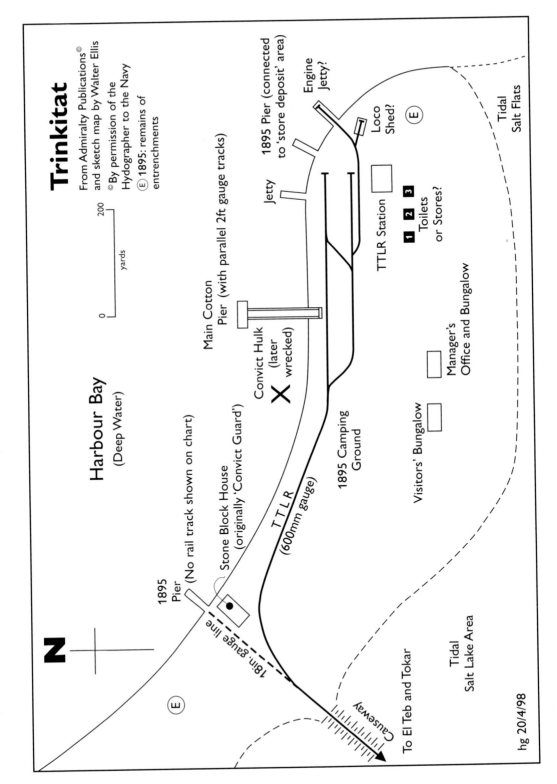

Trinkitat

From Admiralty Publications©
and sketch map by Walter Ellis

© By permission of the
Hydographer to the Navy

Ⓔ 1895: remains of
entrenchments

Harbour Bay
(Deep Water)

N

200

0

yards

1895 Pier
(No rail track shown on chart)

Stone Block House
(originally 'Convict Guard')

Main Cotton
Pier (with parallel 2ft gauge tracks)

Convict Hulk
(later
X wrecked)

1895 Pier (connected
to 'store deposit' area)

Engine
Jetty?

Jetty

Loco
Shed?

Ⓔ

Tidal
Salt Flats

TTLR Station

1 2 3

Toilets
or Stores?

Manager's
Office and Bungalow

1895 Camping
Ground

Visitors' Bungalow

TTLR
(600mm gauge)

18in. gauge line

Ⓔ

To El Teb and Tokar

Tidal
Salt Lake Area

Causeway

hg 20/4/98

Chapter 6

ALONG THE ROUTE FROM TRINKITAT TO TOKAR

"The harbour opens to the north-east, is about $^1/_2$ mile wide, extends $^3/_4$ mile to the southward, has a depth of 4 fathoms, and is capable of accommodating 20 vessels drawing from 18 to 21 feet … The shores of the harbour are sandy, with low bushes." So wrote Count Gleichen of Trinkitat in 1905, quoting from the "Red Sea Pilot", one of the navigation guides produced by the Hydrographer to the Navy to augment information for mariners contained in Admiralty charts. Trinkitat Harbour is covered by Chart 675. Historic editions of this chart, and of the "Red Sea Pilot", consulted at the UK Hydrographic Office by kind permission of the Hydrographer, provided valuable details of the development of port facilities. The accompanying map of Trinkitat (fig. ??) was prepared from Admiralty charts and "Pilots", and from a sketch map prepared from memory by Walter Ellis in the 1980s to show the port area as he remembered it from the 1930s.

In the mid-1890s, Chart 675 indicated signs of naval and military presence at Trinkitat. At the eastern end of the southern shore of the harbour – where later port facilities developed – were a walled "store deposit" area with a small pier, and the remains of an entrenchment. Westwards, in the area where the TLLR terminus was later built, was a camping ground. On the shoreline northwards was a convict hulk, whose skeletal remains lingered until Walter Ellis' time, as discussed below. West of the camping ground was a stone blockhouse near the shore which was marked "convict guard" on the chart. Just beyond the blockhouse, running approximately south-west – north-east was a "causeway and railway to Tokar", with a single track ending on the shoreline at the base of the pier. The remains of another military entrenchment were shown on the chart west of the railway, close to the shore. The 6th (1909) edition of the "Red Sea Pilot" noted: "The railway to Tokar, starting from the south-west shore of the harbour near the stone blockhouse … has been completed, also a small pier at its terminus." Despite these two indications that the 18in. gauge military railway was completed to Tokar, however, there is no other supporting evidence that it was extended beyond El Teb. Admiralty charts and the "Pilots" are primarily focused on navigational matters, and it may have been that marginal information on inland communications from a very minor port was incorrectly received.

In 1921, Storrar found Trinkitat *a desolate, bleak looking spot*", but Williams and his wife later enjoyed the fine local crabs! The port facilities were never extensive. Storrar noted three small jetties, but by the 1940s Sharp wrote of three jetties of steel and timber construction. One was used by steamers and tugs and two were used by the *sambuks*. In addition to the cotton traffic, the *sambuks* handled a good deal of commercial traffic for merchants at Tokar during the periods in the year when the light railway was operational. Sharp reported in 1945 that Trinkitat was very busy at the height of the cotton-shipping season and added that, for the first time that year, cotton was being transported to Suakin and Port Sudan by Sudan Railways tugs and lighters. As the Tokar district cotton crop in 1945 was the heaviest on record, it would provide a good test of the new arrangement.

The 1933 edition of Chart 675 and the 1932 (8th) edition of the "Red Sea Pilot" indicated port facilities in the TTLR era. The "Pilot" noted: "A pier for loading cotton extends about 120 yards northwards, 3 cables (600 yds.) eastward of the stone blockhouse. It has a "T" head 30 yards long with a least depth of 11 feet. A small hauling off buoy is moored close NW of the head of this pier, during the cotton season." This firmly-anchored buoy allowed ships to haul themselves off the pierhead when winds were unfavourable. The "Pilot" continued: "A short unusable jetty lies about half a cable (100 yds.) eastward of the pier and two small jetties with depths of 7 feet alongside their heads, which are used by dhows, lie eastward of this jetty."

Walter's sketch map also showed the main "T" shaped pier with three jetties to the east of it. A single track of the TTLR was shown running onto the easternmost jetty, which he titled the "Engine Jetty". Neither the chart or Walter's map show rail tracks along the main pier. However, in 1934 D. M. Porter took a photograph (now in the Sudan Archive) of the SS TOKAR moored at the end of the "T" shaped pier. This showed two rail tracks, one along either side of the leg of the pier which ran out from the shore. David Ellis explained that these two tracks were laid by Arthur, exactly spaced so that a WDLR bogie chassis could run along them with bogies turned at right angles to their normal positions. A pile driving rig was then mounted on the wagon chassis. TTLR staff maintained the pier and the jetties, a job which required regular attention due the sandy bottom of the harbour. In 1938 piles on the pier needed replacement due to corrosion.

Putting together information from both map sources, the TTLR terminus during the 1930s included a loop, the centre of which was south of the base of the main "T" shaped pier. The chart showed two sidings running eastwards from the southern track of the loop, and Walter's map indicated that the southern siding may have connected to a locomotive shed and the "Engine Jetty". Both sources show a range of buildings in the terminus area. Walter marked a bungalow which combined a local Manager's office (his own) with a living room. The TTLR General Manager's office (i.e. Arthur Ellis' office) was at Tokar. Next door was a two-bedroom Rest House bungalow for the rare visitors, which Williams noted was known as "Honey-moon Villa"! Walter marked three small buildings by the loop as "1, 2 & 3". Were these simply warehouses or stores, or were they passenger waiting rooms or toilets, rigidly differentiated (Colonial style) by Class? Both sources show a station building, which the 1943 chart noted to mariners as having a "conspicuous red roof". Walter also marked an "old fort" to the west, which would have been the stone blockhouse marked on the earlier charts.

To reach firm ground inland, the successive 18in. and 600mm. gauge lines had to run along the causeway from Trinkitat across the tidal harbour and salt lakes. As mentioned earlier, Walter Ellis reckoned that Mumtaz Pasha had used prison labour to build the causeway before 1884. He also thought that an old wrecked ship, whose skeleton lay beached right opposite the Manager's office, was Mumtaz's convict ship which sailed between Suez and Suakin, before running aground at Trinkitat during the 1870s. Whatever its origins, the earlier charts showed a "convict hulk" here, with the nearby blockhouse marked for the "convict guard". The railway route continued across a salt flat area for most of the way to El Teb (7ml.), where the 18in. gauge line had its limited terminus, including the small engine shed where RAMESES was later found. The TTLR had a passing loop and a small, white, box-like station building.

In addition to the remains of the fort, gruesome reminders of the past were skulls and bones of the dead from the Battle of El Teb and the earlier engagements of 1883/84, subsequently exposed by the wind during sandstorms. In 1921 Storrar found graveyards, skeletons and cartridge cases abundant. Walter Ellis reckoned that the Hadendowa had killed about 3000 Egyptian soldiers in the area, and that wind scour had unearthed "hundreds of skeletons all over the battlefield". Local Sudanese people refused to visit the area at night because it was felt to be possessed by "Affrita" (Devil spirits) – it seems unlikely that anyone would choose to visit the area after dark! Just north of El Teb lay the remains of early machinery, apparently dispatched in the 1880s for a cotton ginnery in the Tokar area which was never built, as mentioned in A. B. Wylde's book " '83 to '87 in the Sudan". In 1921 Storrar found "the large and cumbersome pieces of an old fashioned beam engine", which had a cast iron flywheel 15ft in diameter and a beam 16ft long. Further away was a Lancashire boiler 6ft in diameter and 24ft long, which had iron spindles bolted on each end. Storrar wondered whether ropes had been attached to these spindles so that convict labour (housed in the hulk in Trinkitat harbour) could have rolled the boiler along. Walter thought that the boiler had indeed been rolled this way by the convicts – but all the way from Suakin!

Continuing southward from El Teb towards Tokar in 1921, Storrar reported a few sand dunes and hillocks, but the land was otherwise dead flat and still very salty – damp and soft. Walter marked a passing loop named Bashitgow on one of his maps, sited about midway between El Teb and Tokar, dividing the TTLR into three single line sections of roughly 7ml. each. A 1939 Sudan Survey map of the area, provided by Dr H. R. J. Davies of the University of Wales, Swansea, named this area Bashat Gaw. A photograph showed Mrs Ellis, Walter's wife, boating at Bashat Gaw. A Wickham inspection trolley stood in front of the forbiddingly plain, white, box-shaped station

Boating at Bashat Gaw! In front of the forbiddingly plain station building, Mrs Ellis rests in a small dinghy, whilst the Wickham inspection trolley awaits further instructions.

building. In the foreground, Mrs Ellis floated in a small dinghy on a "lake", which was probably only a feature during the rainy season. A serious consequence of rainy seasons was track washouts, one of which was shown in photographs taken by D. M. Porter in November 1933.

As we have seen, however, the real enemy was not water, but sand. Between Bashat Gaw and Tokar on his map, Walter indicated a large belt of sand dunes, "always on the move, caused by gale force winds, half-year East to West; half-year West to East. That section of track was always covered and a new diversion made ... Due to sandstorms covering the track, routes through the dunes curved all over the place." The sand dunes ran for about 4ml. from north to south, right across the route of the TTLR, and extended for many miles to east and west. The scale of the annual sand clearance problem on the TTLR was immense, as indicated by an entry in the SR Annual Report for 1937. "Total amount of dust [sand] removed during the year was 91,719 cubic yards as compared with 31,937 yards in 1936."

In 1921 Storrar found Tokar to be a large township. Central to its life were two markets, one for cotton and the other (the *suk*) for general trading. However, like many such down-to-earth market towns, there was little architectural grandeur. A postcard view of a main street, discovered by Derek Bayliss and captioned "Tokar. Main street and Trinkitat Railways line", shows an irregular line of single-storey market shops, each with double doors but no windows. In contrast, as already mentioned, an elegant mosque was built by craftsmen under the direction of Arthur Ellis. There were also Government Offices, a District Commissioner's House, a hospital and a branch of the Bank of Egypt.

The workshop complex at Tokar, viewed from the top of the signal. The "rail straightening machine shop" lies to the left, beside the main line to Tokar station and cotton market. A Hawthorn Leslie stands at the entrance of the engine shed and the earlier Drewry inspection railcar at the door of the workshop, behind the lift gantry. A "D" class wagon carrying a water tank stands in the third road.

The only signal on the line. By the junction of the main line and the workshop yard at Tokar, a Hawthorn Leslie apparently "has the road" to depart for Trinkitat. The train includes a "D" class wagon loaded with bales, a second carrying a water tank, then three wagons with centre wells which were probably "F" class. The workshop gantry appears behind the train, and on the left is the "rail straightening machine shop".

The TTLR first reached a junction where a line branched off southward to the Tokar depot yard. This contained the engine shed and workshop, beyond which were stores and the offices of the General Manager and Chief Engineer. An Ellis photograph taken inside the workshop showed what appeared to be an oil engine driving a lineshaft, from which machine tools were powered by belting and pulleys. Outside were a lifting gantry and pit, and rail-served fuel and water tanks were nearby. Eastward, across the main line, was the "rail straightening machine shop", together with blacksmith's and carpenter's workshops. By the junction was what Walter called "the one and only signal". This had two opposite-facing arms on one post, controlling traffic to and from the station area. From beside this signal the main line curved eastward towards Tokar station and the cotton loading area, passing an old windmill pump for locomotive water supply, no doubt essential for topping up radiators in internal combustion days. East of the Tokar station building was the cotton loading area, immediately adjacent to the cotton market. Walter's map showed four loading sidings.

After passing the cotton market on the south side, a line curved south along a main street of the *suk*, the general trading market, ending close to the mosque whose construction Arthur had supervised. This line would have provided a direct service for *suk* traders, and an Ellis photograph showed a train in the street being loaded with seed cotton bales. However, during 1937 half a kilometre of track leading to Tokar *suk* was lifted and relaid at the TTLR Tokar depot to provide sidings for use in the connection with the Tokar Sand Clearance. Whether or not the track through the Tokar *suk* was

The street in the Tokar suk (general market) along which a TTLR line ran towards the mosque site. A young onlooker watches seed cotton bales being loaded onto a train hauled by a Hawthorn Leslie. The first "D" class wagon, although partly loaded with bales, retains its sides.

relaid after the Clearance was finished (or relaid to provide a link with the Sand Clearance railway) is not yet known.

Around Tokar spread the cotton growing area. The 1939 Sudan Survey map provided by Dr Davies showed the boundaries of nearly 80 separately named rectangular blocks of land around Tokar, covering a total area of over 400,000 acres. These were presumably agricultural land holdings gazetted by the Government, leased or sold to individual farmers, and devoted in part to growing cotton. In 1921 Storrar estimated that 100,000 acres could be flooded annually for cotton growing, but Sharp recorded that some 54,500 feddan (52,320 acres) were under cotton during the record cropping season of 1944/45.

Sources differ in their estimates of the precise length of the TTLR, but Sharp in the official "Sudan Railways Bulletin" in 1945 quoted a figure of 31km (19.4 miles).

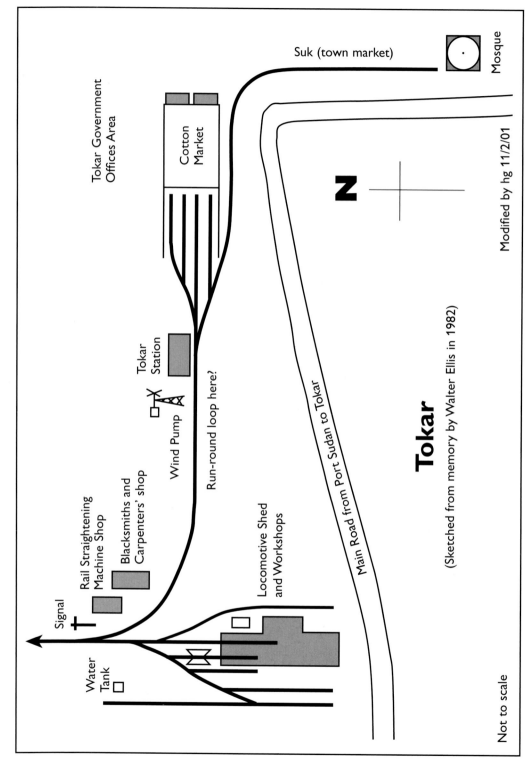

Suk (town market)

Mosque

Tokar Government Offices Area

Cotton Market

Tokar Station

Wind Pump

Run-round loop here?

Rail Straightening Machine Shop

Blacksmiths and Carpenters' shop

Locomotive Shed and Workshops

Signal

Water Tank

Main Road from Port Sudan to Tokar

N

Tokar

(Sketched from memory by Walter Ellis in 1982)

Modified by hg 11/2/01

Not to scale

Chapter 7

A RIDDLE OF THE SANDS –
THE TOKAR SAND CLEARANCE,
1937/38

One of the most fascinating railway documents in the Sudan Archive at the University of Durham was an album of over 160 photographs titled "Tokar sand clearance, 1937–1938. Presented by K. B. el Koussa, contractor, to Mr B. Kennedy Cook, M.C., Governor, Kassala." This was passed to the Archive with other papers from Mr Kennedy-Cooke (as his name is correctly spelt). However, there was a riddle. Whilst the album showed a well-equipped 2ft gauge system transporting large quantities of sand – at or around Tokar as the title implies – there was no sign of TTLR locomotives or rolling stock. Separate Ellis collection photographs showed the locomotives illustrated in this album being unloaded from pontoons at Trinkitat by a TTLR Hawthorn Leslie diesel. The answer to this riddle was found in the entry covering Tokar in the 1938 Annual Report of the Sudan Public Works Department (PWD), kindly provided by Mrs Jane Hogan of the Sudan Archive. "The main task of the department at Tokar," it began, "was the clearing away of vast accumulations of sand which threatened to engulf the town." Since 1921 there had been change in the annual flood pattern of the Khor Baraka. Coupled with the effects of the sand-bearing winds – the *haboob* from the south-west and the *hababai* from the north-east – this had resulted in huge sand dunes *(debba)* close to the town. These in turn intercepted more wind-blown sand, increasing their size.

It was decided to transport the sand by light railway, wagons being loaded and unloaded manually. 550 Saidis, who Hill respectfully described as "Upper Egyptian workmen with a prodigious reputation for earth-moving" were employed for the job, leaving local workers to concentrate on the cotton crop. The light railway imported by the PWD was of considerable proportions. "The main plant included 2 diesel locomotives of 74hp. and 1 of 55hp., 4 Simplex locomotives of 40hp., 350 tip wagons, 50 5 cubic metre wagons, and 7.5 miles of decauville track. Engine sheds, workshop and stores were erected for their maintenance." There was, however, a considerable job to do. Nearly 900,000 cubic metres of sand were removed from the western half of a *debba* "... which cleared the town up to the mosque area ... All material excavated was deposited south-east of the town at an approximate distance of 1 mile. The average output was approximately 6000 cubic metres per day." The activities of the Sand Clearance railway seem therefore to have been concentrated on the eastern side of

Tokar Sand Clearance, 1937/38. A fine indication of the scale of the job, and of the debba (dune) which had to be moved. A Drewry stands at the head of a train which includes all three types of bogie wagon. The first bogie wagon is of the all-steel high-ended type. The rest of the train is made up of the wooden and steel sided designs, both descended from the WDLR "D" class. Workmen take a sensible rest from the sun in the shade of V-skips in the foreground.

Tokar. The full role which the TTLR played in the Clearance has not yet been discovered. The 1937 SR Annual Report noted that "a half kilometre of track leading to Tokar Suk was pulled up and relaid at Tokar depot for use in connection with the dust clearance scheme to be undertaken by the Public Works Department." No doubt extra sidings were needed to accommodate the large influx of rolling stock and other equipment for the Clearance, all of which presumably came by sea to Trinkitat. One Ellis collection photograph shows an "eleven locomotive train", with a TTLR Hawthorn Leslie at the head of ten recently-landed Clearance locomotives.

Details of the rail link between the Clearance system and the TTLR at Tokar have yet to be discovered. A photograph from the 1937/38 Clearance album appeared on page 455 of "Continental Railway Journal" No. 96 in an article on Khartoum trams. It was captioned there as showing a TTLR Hawthorn Leslie diesel at work, which was not correct. The view was of a Clearance railway Drewry diesel at the head of a long train of V-skips, running along a tree-lined street. This would imply that the link between the two systems passed through Tokar. The PWD Annual Report mentioned sand clearance near the mosque. Maybe a link was provided by relaying track along the former TTLR route which ran through the *suk* to the mosque site (from which rails had been lifted to provide sidings) once extra supplies of permanent way material for the Clearance system had arrived at Tokar.

Another published view of the Clearance rail system was also incorrectly captioned. That was a photograph in Hill's "Sudan Transport" captioned "TTLR: shed staff and engines, Tokar, around 1949." Close study, however, reveals that buildings differ from those at the TTLR Tokar depot which appear in Ellis photographs, and the locomotives on view are those supplied for the Clearance. This was certainly a 1937/38 view, which appears to show the Clearance railway locomotive shed and workshop at Tokar.

No less than eleven internal combustion locomotives seem to have been used on the job, according to Clearance album and Ellis photographs. The two diesels of 74hp. and one of 55hp., mentioned in the 1938 PWD Annual Report, were built by English Electric for Drewry; they were supplied new to the Sudan PWD. The four 40hp. Simplexes, also mentioned in the Annual Report, appeared in photographs with the "post war" superstructure styling. Although not specifically mentioned in the Annual Report, three small Howard petrol locomotives and an Orenstein & Koppel diesel also appear in photographs. The histories of these locomotives before and after the Clearance are shrouded in mystery. The Drewrys were certainly large locomotives for run-of-the-mill construction jobs for which Decauville-type light railway equipment might have been used elsewhere in the Sudan.

Tokar Sand Clearance, 1937/38. Four Simplexes, two six-coupled Drewrys (with their upper cab sides still stacked on front footplates), and the four-coupled Drewry, apparently fully assembled.

Tokar Sand Clearance, 1937/38. Four trains of V-skips, 350 of which were provided for the job. Motive power, from the left: Simplex, Drewry, Simplex, Drewry. Note variations in skip bucket shapes.

Slight design differences amongst the many V-skips shown in the Clearance album photographs indicate that they may have come from a number of builders. The wagons of five cubic metre capacity which appear in album photographs were of three bogie designs, all updated successors to the WDLR "D" class. Details of these wagons, and of the eleven Clearance locomotives, appear in the section on locomotives and rolling stock.

Chapter 8

NARROW GAUGE IN THE DOCKS
AT PORT SUDAN

A narrow gauge system within the docks at Port Sudan was mentioned by Pole in his 1924 Report on the SR. "In addition to the standard [3ft 6in.] gauge railways on the quay, a narrow gauge equipment has been introduced and three petrol locomotives and 57 vehicles are now in use." He warned that although such a system, presumably of 2ft gauge, could be useful for transport purely within the docks complex, warehouses should not be established which were only served by the narrow gauge track. No mention of this "narrow gauge" system appeared in the SR Annual Report for 1924, nor in Hill's "Sudan Transport". As to the three petrol locomotives, Rodney Weaver advised that in December 1925 Motor Rail processed a spares order for three ex-WDLR 40hp. Simplexes belonging to Sudan Government Railways. However, the Motor Rail works numbers in that order did not match those linked to the WDLR running numbers of the TTLR locomotives (see section on TTLR Simplexes below). Any rail system at Port Sudan would almost certainly have been owned by Sudan Railways, whereas it is likely that in the 1920s the TTLR locomotives belonged to the contractors, Vincent and Ellis, to whom spares would have been consigned. A logical conclusion, therefore, is that the three Simplexes identified by Weaver were the three noted by Pole at Port Sudan, although no other details of the "narrow gauge" system there have yet been discovered.

Chapter 9

LOCOMOTIVES
AND ROLLING STOCK

18 INCH GAUGE LOCOMOTIVES AND ROLLING STOCK

VULCAN and MERCURY at Suakin

It is not intended to cover in detail the 18in. gauge equipment used around Suakin in 1884/85, as much information is already available in Smithers' book. VULCAN and MERCURY (VF 939 of 1883 and 1075 of 1884) were 0-4-2 tanks, with their water supply of 200 gallons stored on either side of the footplate. Smithers reproduced an 1883 drawing of VULCAN, which was designed by Major Thomas English, R.E., and fitted with the English Patent Trailing Truck (Patent No. 3869 of 1883). This comprised a longitudinal crankshaft which compressed the suspension spring to apply side control when a curve was being negotiated. The builders obviously wished to publicise English's patent as Chris Veitch found a drawing of the very similar MARS and VENUS (VF 1160/61 of 1885) in "The Engineer" of 31 July 1885. This was titled "Inventions Exhibition – Swivel Bogie Locomotive. The Vulcan Foundry Company, Newton-le-Willows, constructors." From the 1883 drawing of VULCAN, the cylinders were 7.5in. by 12in. and all wheels of 1ft 8in. diameter. Coupled and total wheelbases were of 3ft and 7ft 6in. Gross weight was 10 tons, total heating surface area 210 sq.ft and the "radius of curve traversable at low speed" 50ft. As already mentioned, Smithers concluded that VULCAN and MERCURY returned to Britain after the Suakin-Berber Railway fiasco.

The Fowlers and Bagnalls which never reached Suakin

Only brief mention will be made of the seven Fowler and five Bagnall locomotives ordered for use at Suakin, but never delivered there due to the sudden demise of the Suakin-Berber Railway. The Fowlers were 0-4-2s with long side tanks and Smithers noted that they were also designed by Major English. They were dimensionally similar to the Vulcan locomotives just described and their works numbers were 5058-64 of 1885. They sported the names of birds (some found in the Sudan): CORMORANT, VULTURE, OSTRICH, QUAIL, OWL, FLAMINGO and PELICAN.

The five Bagnall 0-4-2 tanks took their names from Ancient Egypt: SERAPIS, OSIRIS, ANUBIS, ISIS and APIS. They were ordered in February 1885, and carried works numbers 710-14. Baker noted that the first two were finished in June 1885 and the last three in August 1885; also that two Bagnall registers placed OSIRIS as 710 and

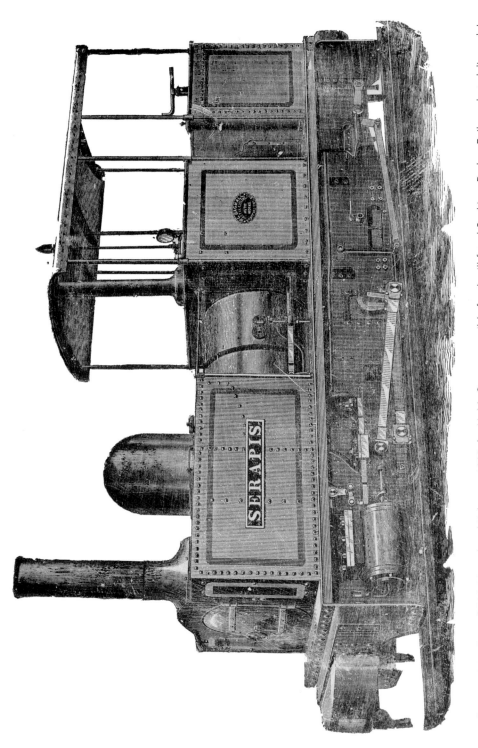

Bagnall 711/1885 – One of 710-14, ordered February 1885, by H. M. Gout, ostensibly for the ill fated Suakin – Berber Railway, but delivered June 1885 to Woolwich Arsenal, and they apparently spent their entire lives there. 710 was rebuilt at Stafford July 1894: 714 received a new copper firebox in October 1905.

SERAPIS as 711. Although these Bagnalls never reached Suakin, their design was a predecessor to that of RAMESES (another Ancient Egyptian). They were inverted saddle tanks (IST), and Baker recorded that each weighed 10.5 tons in working order. Other dimensions were: cylinders 7.5in. x 12in., driving wheels 2ft 0.75in., wheelbase 3ft 6in. They had copper fireboxes and brass tubes. Stephenson link motion was fitted between the (outside) frames, actuating valves placed on top of the outside cylinders via rocking shafts. Baker presumed that the narrowness of the gauge prevented the valves being in the conventional place for a locomotive with inside gear. Smithers described the valve gear as Stephenson/Howe link motion, and Baker and Civil recorded that they cost £565 each. Robertson in his 1898 paper "Narrow gauge railways – two feet and under" commented that these Bagnalls were "found to be rather apt to leave the rails, the bogie [i.e. rear truck] arrangement not being entirely satisfactory for the work". W. G. Bagnall responded in a Written Contribution to the discussion of the paper that "another bogie [design] had been preferred to that which he had proposed to supply; it was a new design, and had at that time been thought by the authorities as an improvement". Was that design Major English's "Patent Trailing Truck", as had been fitted to the Vulcan Foundry locomotives mentioned above?

RAMESES on the 1896 military railway to El Teb

Baker recorded that RAMESES (WB 1452) was ordered on 19 January, 1896 as "one 8 inch locomotive, can altered, nameplate 'RAMESES', 1ft 6in. gauge". It was

RAMESES, the Bagnall 0-4-0 IST of the 18-inch gauge military railway in 1921/22, after excavation from the locomotive shed site at El Teb. It was presumably loaded onto a TTLR "D" class wagon for transport to Trinkitat, after which it apparently went to the S. R. Atbara Workshops for scrapping. Arthur Ellis, with cummerbund, stands on the left beside a "D" class wagon fitted with end stanchions.

despatched to E. H. M. Leggett, FOB Liverpool on 17 February of the same year at the cost of £546 5s 0d. Baker also noted that one register gave the customer as the Egyptian Government. It was an 0-4-0IST without the trailing truck of the Suakin order. Smithers considered it very similar to the 18in. gauge AJAX (WB 1442), despatched to Woolwich Arsenal in January 1895. The design of AJAX was discussed in an article titled "RENOWN" by Roger West in "Industrial Railway Record" No. 90. An engraving and description of an 18in. gauge Bagnall 0-4-0IST named RENOWN appeared in "The Engineer" for 26 January 1894, but no locomotive to that precise design was ever built. However, West noted similarities with AJAX, and with a 3ft 6in. gauge Bagnall IST, "No. 2" of the London Country Council's Northern Outfall Sewage Works, Beckton (WB 1424 of 1893). There were also differences. Neither AJAX or RAMESES featured Baguley's valve gear, which No. 2 and the RENOWN engraving did. AJAX and RENOWN had a dropped footplate, which No. 2 and RAMESES did not. The three 18in. gauge locomotives all had outside frames.

Baker and Civil noted that when Ernest Edwin Baguley had joined Bagnall from Hawthorn Leslie in 1891, he brought new ideas to the design office. RENOWN was proposed as a modified 18in. gauge 0-4-0IST design with Baguley's valve gear. However, AJAX, and subsequently RAMESES, were delivered without it. Did Woolwich military thinking prevail over the innovative ideas of Baguley, as in the case of the 0-4-2 trailing truck design which Bagnall said had been forced upon him in 1885? Further points from Robertson's 1898 paper are relevant. He mentions that four classes of 18in. gauge locomotives were in daily use at Woolwich Arsenal, although those four classes did not include all the 18in. gauge locomotives at Woolwich at the time. The first three were Hudswell Clarke 0-4-0ST, Bagnall 0-4-2IST (as discussed above) and Manning Wardle 0-4-0ST. The fourth class was "Bagnall's Ajax engines, built specially for the War Office and to their designs". In his Written Contribution response, W. G. Bagnall commented that the Ajax engines "had been built specially for the War Office from his own designs, with the exception of one or two brasses which had been made duplicates of those in other engines running there".

The references to "Bagnall's Ajax engines" in the plural are of interest, for after AJAX, RAMESES was the only 18in. gauge Bagnall 0-4-0IST to be supplied to the War Office. However, thirteen locomotives built by Bagnall at around the same time as AJAX and RAMESES were also 0-4-0IST for military use, supplied to the Gibraltar Dockyard (WB 1447-51 of 1895 and 1467-74 of 1895/96). Although of metre gauge, they had identical cylinder and driving wheel dimensions to RAMESES. Maybe this 0-4-0IST design was classified by Bagnall as their "Ajax" type. Was it coincidental that a Bagnall 2ft gauge 0-4-0IST supplied in 1895 to the Nine Elms Works of the Gas, Light and Coke Co. in London (WB 1460) also carried the name "AJAX"?

Baker and Civil recorded that RAMESES had 8in. by 12in. cylinders and 2ft 0.5in. driving wheels. The Gibraltar Dockyard Bagnalls had the same sized cylinders and wheels and a 3ft 6in. wheelbase. Their heating surface area was 135 sq. ft (tubes) and 19.5 sq. ft (firebox), grate area 3.5 sq. ft, working pressure 140 psi. In working order, they carried 230 gallons of water and had fuel storage of 10 cu. ft. Copper fireboxes and brass tubes were fitted. AJAX had 7in. by 12in. cylinders, 2ft 1in. wheels, 3ft 3in. wheelbase, 114 sq. ft. of tube heating surface, a grate area of 3.2sq. ft and cost £475.

There is no record of any locomotive other than RAMESES operating on the 18in. gauge military railway, and no details survive of its solitary existence there. Arthur Ellis photographed the resurrected Bagnall loaded onto a 600mm. gauge WDLR bogie wagon chassis around the time the TTLR was opened in 1922. RAMESES was apparently then taken away to the main Sudan Railways Atbara Workshops and probably scrapped soon afterwards.

Wagons at Suakin and Trinkitat

No precise details of the 18in. gauge wagons used around Suakin and on the line to El Teb have so far been discovered. At Suakin, Capt. Kunhardt referred to "two trucks with four 500 gallon tanks of water" being a realistic limit for VENUS and MERCURY. Smithers reproduced a drawing, from the Royal Engineer's Committee Extracts for 1881, of an 18in. gauge bogie "dual purpose gun/stores trolley with removable sides". With internal dimensions of 12ft long by 4ft wide, two 500gl. tanks placed on such a trolley would each have been around 3ft 6in. high. An alternative vehicle could have been the "18-inch gauge bogie wagon for general use, designed and constructed by the Lancaster Wagon Company" for use on the Chatham Fortifications, of which Smithers also reproduced a drawing, dating from around 1882. This design was 18ft long internally, so two 500gl. water tanks taking up the full floor area would be proportionately shallower, around 2ft 6in. high, making the wagon more stable.

Chapter 10

LOCOMOTIVES
AND ROLLING STOCK ON THE
TOKAR-TRINKITAT LIGHT RAILWAY

Orenstein & Koppel steam locomotives

There is no clear evidence as to origins of the five 30hp. 0-4-0 O & K steam locomotives with which, as Hill noted, the TTLR started operation. An Ellis photograph, reproduced in "Sudan Transport", showed four of them, two with cab backplates and two without, probably outside the shed at Tokar. Hill dated the photograph "about 1921". The O & Ks looked in a poor state, without coupling or connecting rods. Hill added that three were scrapped in 1922. Useful material from the "Orenstein & Koppel Steam Locomotives Works List, 1892-1945" by Fricke, Bude and Murray has been quoted by Weaver. Apparently forty 30hp. well tanks were sent to Arthur Koppel's Cairo depot as stock during 1905 to 1907, one of which was sold on to Argentina as late as 1920. John Browning's fascinating article "A military mystery tour" in "Industrial Railway Record" No. 141 indicated that a number of O & K 600mm. gauge 0-4-0 tanks were "acquired" by Australian and British forces during the

The four Orenstein & Koppel 0-4-0 well tanks with which the TTLR started operations, all looking rather the worse for wear. Possibly at Tokar depot, or at the (as yet unidentified) site where they operated before purchase for use on the TTLR. If they were in this sorry state at Tokar, had the fifth locomotive done all the construction work required to build the railway from Trinkitat?

First World War from local industrial users in Egypt. Could any of these have been sold on to the TTLR? Research published in "Continental Railway Journal" No. 96 on O & K locomotives used on the Khartoum steam trams indicated that these were mainly 0-4-2 tanks, as were other O & K steam tanks recorded by John Browning. However, two 30hp. 0-4-0 tanks, works numbers 1177 and 1179 of 1903, were apparently Nos 1 and 2 of the Khartoum tram system.

Motor Rail Simplexes on the TTLR – and at Port Sudan?

Much of the rolling stock used on the TTLR came from the First World War Department Light Railways, and helpful information has come from "Light railways of the First World War" by W. J. K. Davies, "Railways and war before 1918" by Dennis Bishop and Davies and the 1987 and 1996 volumes titled "Narrow gauge at war" by Keith Taylorson. Also "The Light Track from Arras" by T. R. Heritage. Of the four 40hp. Simplexes which Hill reported as arriving on the TTLR in 1922, Walter Ellis wrote later: "When I started there in 1930 it was still petrol. Locos were "Simplex", 4 wheels driven on front and rear axles by chain links from a centre gearbox. Three speed forward and 3 speed reverse ... They were originally built covered with armoured plating, but sides and part of roof had to be removed as it got too **hot** due to Sudan's excessive hot climate. Chains got a **lot** of sand on them, which with gear oil on the chain drive to both axles made a good grinding paste. We used to **boil** the chains in order to get the grease and grit out. So we used up a lot of chains." Taylorson added that the engines were Dorman 4JO four cylinder units, and that Dixon-Abbott two speed gearboxes were fitted.

As to the armoured plating, the WDLR 40hp. Simplexes had three types of superstructure, all of which had heavy curved steel sheet covers at each end. The "open" type had a simple four-pillar canopy cab roof. The "protected" type could be closed in by steel side doors and visors below the roof line. The "armoured" type was entirely enclosed, like a small rail-mounted tank. From photographs, the Simplexes ran on the TTLR in "open" style, with simple four-pillar roofs. In addition, the curved steel sheet covers had been removed from one end of each locomotive, no doubt to assist cooling, as noted by Walter. At some stage one (WDLR running number 2190) acquired a new roof canopy which extended the length of the locomotive, curving across it like that on earlier designs of Wickham inspection railcars. It appears to have been the only one so modified. Another modification resulted in large "steps" being attached to the sides of the frames at each end of the Simplexes, possibly for shunters to ride on when trains were being marshalled.

Ellis photographs showed the WDLR running numbers of all four TTLR Simplexes, and tables in the books by Davies and Taylorson allow these to be linked both to Motor Rail works numbers and to body "types" as built. This has been done in the table below. For the TTLR Simplexes, the WDLR running numbers visible in

Ellis photographs have been combined with data from Taylorson. In most cases it has been possible to confirm these identities from surviving Motor Rail records.

Railway	MR Works no.	Date Ex-Works	WDLR no.	*Body type
TTLR	405	19-7-1917	2126	open
	422	17-8-1917	2143	open
	469	26-3-1918	2190	armoured
	513	20-12-1917	2234	protected
?Port Sudan	439	7-9-1917	2160	open
	453	21-9-1917	2174	open
	573	20-2-1918	2294	protected

* Body type as built, according to the records discussed.

The traumatic operating conditions of the First World War could have meant that each original chassis and superstructure did not always stay together. Taylorson noted that Motor Rail produced kits which allowed "open" type Simplexes to be upgraded to "armoured" or "protected" types. With the "open" type being most popular for postwar civilian use, it was presumably not difficult to reverse this process. The "armoured" 40hp. Simplex illustrated in the book by Bishop and Davies carries the WDLR running number 2143, noted in the table above as originally assigned to an "open" type. Further detective work on the TTLR Simplexes could make use of such details as the positions of exhaust pipes and WDLR number plates.

A most interesting modification was that, in later life, one of the TTLR Simplexes was modified by the SR so that the Dorman engine could run on fuel gas generated from the burning of charcoal. A photograph exists of this locomotive after the conversion, but before the wheels were re-fitted, possibly taken at the main SR Atbara Workshops. A full length roof was fitted, so it was probably WDLR 2190. A hopper at roof level, which presumably held the charcoal, was mounted above what looked like a combustion chamber (with centrifugal fan). Long tubes across the other end of the locomotive probably contained filters for "scrubbing" the fuel gas before it was fed to the Dorman engine. The whole exercise may have taken place during the fuel-short days of the Second World War. Possibly the TTLR Simplex had already been withdrawn, and was simply used as a fixed test rig in this form to demonstrate the practicality of the idea. The almost total absence of trees in any of the Ellis photographs indicated that the Tokar area was not a likely source of charcoal.

Hawthorn Leslie diesels

Details of the TTLR Hawthorn Leslie 0-4-0 diesels came from Walter Ellis' notes, an article in the Supplement to "The Railway Gazette" for February 24, 1933 (Walter's

A charcoal-burning Simplex! Sudan Railways experimented with converting one of the TTLR Simplexes (possibly WDLR 2190) so that its Dorman engine would run on gases generated by burning charcoal. This view, possibly at the S. R. Atbara Workshops, appears to show the converted locomotive before the wheels were restored. Charcoal was presumably stored in the roof hopper on the right, and then fed into a fuel gas generation chamber below. An air flow to help generate fuel gas could have been provided by the fan just above the frame on the extreme right. The tubular structures to the left were most likely for cleaning (or "scrubbing") the fuel gases before they were fed to the engine unit.

copy) and coverage in Brian Webb's "The British Internal Combustion Locomotive: 1894-1940". The first two (HL 3808/9) were ordered on 16 September 1932, to a gauge of 2ft (as we have seen). They were allotted SR running numbers 55/6, and were delivered in February 1933. According to Eric Maxwell, the third locomotive (HL 3835) was ordered on 14 May 1934, and delivered as SR No. 57. Webb considered the locomotives to be of quite straightforward design. They were powered by six-cylinder, cold starting airless-injection McLaren M.D.B. six-cylinder diesel engines, developing 90 bhp. at 800 rpm. Transmission was via a David Brown multiplate clutch and a three-speed gearbox (of HL's special design), then through David Brown worm reduction gear to the jackshaft. Speeds were 3.3, 6.6 and 10 mph. HL were amongst the first

The two original TTLR Hawthorn Leslies SR 56 and 55, and three Simplexes on a train of "D" and "F" class wagons, almost certainly at Trinkitat. The HLs have no round spectacles in their cab fronts, so the date must have been soon after their arrival in 1933. The Simplexes have extra "steps" attached to the frames, and the third (probably WDLR 2190) has an extended roof.

builders to adopt worm reduction gear for rail traction purposes. Driving wheel diameters were 2ft 4in. and the wheelbase was 5ft. Sharp noted that they weighed 9 tons, and were 16ft 10in. long, 5ft 6in. wide and 10ft high.

Hawthorn Leslie put considerable effort into producing a design for operation in a sandy, tropical climate. A JAP V-twin petrol engine was used for starting, driving a friction roller off the main engine flywheel. Walter Ellis noted that electrical or compressed air starting would have been unsuitable for sandy dust storm conditions. The cooling system comprised a Reliance radiator and auxiliary water tank, with a combined capacity of 50gl. When the first two arrived at Trinkitat, however, Walter was not happy with them. Hawthorn Leslie, he noted, "made some vital errors, some of which I had altered when [the SR] sent the order for the third locomotive. Herein their errors ..." First on the list was the gauge problem, already discussed. Then came the fitting of open type oil boxes to wheel axle bearings, despite the severe sand and dust conditions. A solid centre cab front plate meant that the driver could not see straight ahead, so Walter had portholes fitted, also slatted sun-shutters and an insulated cab roof. Acetylene lamps replaced "feeble, useless" paraffin ones, and backs were fitted to the cab steps to prevent feet slipping and being caught and severely damaged by the coupling rod from the jackshaft. The third locomotive, SR 57, incorporated many of Walter's modifications, as well as having a wider footplate and cab. "Also instead of a stupid little feeble KLAXON hand push horn I made them fit a good whistle operated by the exhaust so one could pull it to warn animals and people well ahead or behind."

A works photograph of SR 57 appears in Webb's book, and both the first two HLs were subsequently modified to incorporate some of Walter's design suggestions. Thus modified, they lasted very well under the severe conditions of the TTLR. After closure in 1952 two of them continued operation for their new owners, the Sudan Gezira Board, as reported in "Diesel Operation in The Sudan", an article in "Diesel Railway Traction" for November 1953, brought to light by David Brewer. A final point, already mentioned, is that the diesel at the head of a train of V-skips illustrated in an article on Khartoum trams on page 455 of "Continental Railway Journal" No. 96 is not one of these TTLR Hawthorn Leslies, but Drewry DC 2083 at work on the Tokar Sand Clearance.

Wagons on the TTLR

As already noted, most wagons used to transport seed cotton bales on the TTLR were of the WDLR "D" class, which were produced by a number of different British builders. The steel end stanchions fitted to retain cotton bales have already been described. Wagon sides were generally removed for transporting seed cotton bales, as the bales were too long to fit comfortably across the wagons with the sides in position. Wagons without sides were also used for transporting water tanks, continuing the tradition of the 18in. gauge line. Sides were re-fitted for sand clearing and general transport work. The special "D" class wagons modified for carrying passengers, and for braking trains hauled by the HL diesels, have already been described. In addition to the "D" class, Ellis photographs showed similar wagons with storage wells between the bogies. Two WDLR wagon designs had this feature, the "well" being a wooden sided open-topped storage box sunk between the bogies, supported by a sub-frame. One design was the "E" class, which had wooden planked sides like a "D" class, but drop doors only above the storage well. The sides above the bogies were fixed. Illustrated coverage of this design appears in the Gratton and Band Ashover book. The other design was the "F" class, which had no sides. Metal sockets were attached to the sides and ends of the floor, into which removable stanchions could be fitted to retain bulky loads. Comparison of Ellis photographs of TTLR wagons with a view of an "F" class wagon in the book by Bishop and Davies indicated close similarities. No TTLR photograph showed the removable stanchions originally supplied with these wagons, although Arthur Ellis had fitted them with fixed end stanchions to retain cotton bales. One Ellis view showed extra seed cotton bales being loaded into the storage well, before the "normal" load of 24 bales was added above floor level.

A third type of WDLR bogie wagon used, most noticeable in photographs of the construction of the TTLR, appears to have been the "C" class, some of which had

"All hands" loading a seed cotton bale, complete with a casual passenger! The wagon on the right has a centre well, into which bales seem to have been loaded. It was almost certainly a WDLR "F" class, as sockets are visible along its sides into which removable stanchions could be fitted for First World War operational use. Fixed steel end stanchions have been added by Arthur Ellis to retain cotton bales.

TTLR Simplex WDLR 2190, with a train of seed cotton bales and "passengers". The rear end sheet of the Simplex has been removed due to the hot Sudanese climate. In later views 2190 appears with an overall roof canopy. Ropes to retain cotton bales are attached to steel rings at the tops of the vertical stanchions at the ends of the wagons. The second wagon retains its sides, although the bales do not seem to lie comfortably across a wagon with sides in position.

completely removable sides and ends. Davies noted that the "C" class had been derived from four-wheeled wagon designs, and were themselves overtaken late in 1916 by the new, longer "D", "E" and "F" class wagons. Another component of the TTLR rolling stock fleet was a collection of four-wheeled contractors type V-skips, much needed for sand clearing operations.

TTLR inspection railcars

There seem to have been two inspection railcars on the TTLR, no doubt used primarily for senior management transport. The history of these vehicles has yet to be researched. The earlier vehicle, numbered "TTLR No. 1", looks very much like a Drewry/Baguley product. The later one, a Wickham, had a jack and swivel system under the body to allow it to be moved onto short track lengths at right angles to the main line. It was delivered with a four-wheeled trailer, which carried what looks like a tool box/bench seat, together with handrails for those riding on it.

Chapter 11

LOCOMOTIVES
AND ROLLING STOCK ON THE
TOKAR SAND CLEARANCE

Drewry/English Electric diesels

In 1936/37, three 2ft gauge Drewry/English Electric locomotives were supplied to the Sudan Government Public Works Department. Weaver recorded that these were two 0-6-0s with 74hp. Gardner 6L2 engines (DC 2075/EE 919 of 1936 and DC 2079/EE 943 of 1937), plus a smaller 0-4-0 with a 50hp. 4L2 engine (DC 2083/ EE 1077 of 1937). The first of the three (DC 2075) was displayed by Drewry at an exhibition in Johannesburg before sale to the Sudan PWD. These three locomotives played a major part in the Clearance, and they are indicated by engine horsepower, although not by the builder, in the 1938 PWD Annual Report. Photographs show that they seem to have been delivered new to Trinkitat, with the upper cab structures stacked on front footplates, for onward transit to Tokar over the TTLR.

A six-coupled Drewry for the Tokar Sand Clearance soon after arrival by pontoon at Trinkitat in 1937. The upper cab structure lies on the front footplate. This view and others indicate that the Drewrys were delivered new to Trinkitat, although they ended their days on a 950mm gauge line in Eritrea.

The design was descended from a standard gauge 0-4-0 diesel, built in 1933 at the English Electric works at Preston for Drewry (works numbers DC 2047/EE 847). With a distinctive sloping bonnet, this was one of eight locomotives supplied by different builders to the London Midland and Scottish Railway for comparative trials of diesel shunters. From being LMS 7050, it later passed into Army use, and was described in some detail by G. Arnott in an article "ARMY 240" in "Industrial Railway Record" No. 50. Like LMS 7050, Sudan PWD locomotives had Wilson-Drewry epicyclic gearboxes and jackshaft drive. What use the Sudan PWD found for these Drewrys after the Clearance is not yet clear. As noted earlier, they were large to operate in the style of small 20hp. locomotives on temporary construction work tracks.

The three Drewrys did not end their lives in the Sudan, however. They were regauged to 950mm. for military use in Eritrea during the Second World War. Hill noted that when the Allied Forces advancing in Eritrea reached the Italian 950mm. gauge railway they found that the Italians had withdrawn their rolling stock as they retreated. The SR Atbara Workshops therefore converted what Hill called three "Drewery diesel decauville locomotives" and some wagons to fit the Italian gauge. Hill added that the Drewrys proved extremely robust in Eritrea. "One was charged by a ten-ton lorry, knocked over, righted, and thereupon continued work as though nothing had happened ..." Eritrea became part of Ethiopia in 1952, and the 950mm. gauge line was described (under the title "Northern Ethiopia Railway") by Bowen, Kalla-Bishop and Lera in articles titled "Railways of Ethiopia" in issues 27 and 29 of the "Continental Railway Journal". Two of the three Sudan PWD Drewry works numbers, 2075 and 2083, appear in their locomotive list. These were both listed as being built in 1937, and as carrying "1939 numbers" of N1 and N3 respectively. However, as the Drewrys did not arrive from the Sudan until later in the War, the dating of those Eritrean numbers cannot be correct. The third Drewry works number in the Eritrean list, DC 2037, was linked to a 1937-built 0-6-0 diesel, for which no Eritrean running number was listed. This was not the works number of the third Sand Clearance locomotive, which was DC 2079. Amazingly, in October 1997 Mike Cunningham and others found three Drewry diesels still existing in Eritrea, two 0-6-0s carrying DC builder's plates 2075 of 1936 and 2078 of 1937 plus 0-4-0 2083 of 1937. The first and third numbers directly match those given by Weaver for the Sudan PWD Drewrys. As to 2078, it can only be noted that it is much closer to the Sudan Drewry number of 2079 than the earlier quoted Eritrean Drewry number of 2037, which could have been a copying error as the date also ended in "37". Hill's comments on the toughness of the Sudan Drewrys were still valid. Cunningham's group found that one 0-6-0 was in working order at Asmara in October 1997 and that the 0-4-0, although under repair, had recently been running a commuter service across the causeway at Massawa, using two converted low-sided wagons. Arthur and Walter Ellis would no doubt have approved!

An eleven locomotive train! During 1937, the third TTLR Hawthorn Leslie, SR 57, stands at the head of no less than ten new arrivals for the Tokar Sand Clearance. Four Simplexes with "post-war" superstructures lead three Drewrys and three small Howards.

Tokar Sand Clearance, 1937/38. A Simplex heads a train of V-skips at the sand unloading point.

Motor Rail Simplex Locomotives

Four 40hp. Simplexes appeared in a photograph of a "train" of ten Clearance locomotives, together with the three Drewrys and three small Howards, shortly after their arrival at Trinkitat in 1937. Their bodywork was of the post-war Motor Rail design, with flat roof panels sloping down from a crossways ridge, and flat sloping panels forming the tops of box-shaped ends. This contrasted with the curved end panels and roofs of the WDLR Simplexes. The frames look similar to those of the WDLR 40hp. designs, however, and a number of First World War 40hp. locomotives were overhauled by Motor Rail and re-sold with the new style bodywork fitted.[1] In the 1938 PWD Annual Report "four Simplex locomotives of 40hp." are specifically mentioned which are presumably the locomotives illustrated. Unfortunately there are at least eight, if not ten, candidates for this quartet. In October 1925 Robert Hudson Ltd. ordered five of these locomotives (works nos. 3814 to 3818 of 1925) for shipment to Port Sudan and three more of the same type (MR 4162 to 4164) were shipped to Port Sudan in late October 1926 to the order of the Sudan Government's Inspecting Engineer in London. All these were probably Sudan PWD stock but there were two more of this type ordered by the London office of the Orient Co. Ltd. and shipped to Port Sudan on 14th December, 1926 (MR 4168) and 15th November, 1927 (MR4202) which are also possible candidates.

Howard petrol "S" type locomotives

Although not specifically mentioned in the 1938 PWD Annual Report, photographs of Clearance locomotives arriving at Trinkitat also showed three small machines by J. & F. Howard of Bedford. Andrew Neale, using information provided by Chris

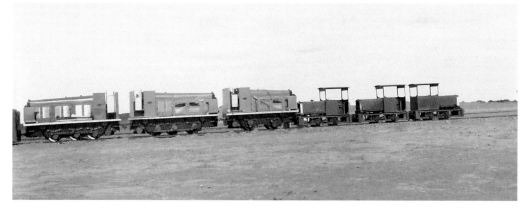

Locomotives for the Tokar Sand Clearance, soon after arrival by pontoon at Trinkitat during 1937. The two six-coupled and one four-coupled Drewrys, and three small four-wheeled Howards.

---

[1] It is unclear from Motor Rail records if such locos were entirely new or simply a rebuild of a former 40 h.p. WDLR loco.

Tokar Sand Clearance, 1937/38. The mystery Orenstein & Koppel diesel and a Simplex at the head of a train of bogie wagons whose design is descended from the WDLR "D" class. The first two wagons have wooden sides; the following two are all-steel, with box-section reinforcing along the tops of the sides.

Fisher, advised that three 20hp. petrol locomotives were supplied in 1929 by Howard to the order of E. J. Allen and Co., who were the London-based import agents for Chile and the Sudan. Howard 954 and 955 (of 2ft gauge) were ex-works in July 1929, and 962 (of 600mm. gauge) in the following month. They were of Howard's "S" type, a four-wheeled design fitted with Morris I.M. (Industrial Marine) engines and weighing 3 tons. They had 18in. wheels and a wheelbase of 3ft 3in. More details appeared in Webb's book. It seems likely that these Howards were ordered for the PWD, and that they were the three locomotives used on the Clearance. Where they operated before or after that job is not at present known.

Orenstein & Koppel Diesel Locomotive

An unidentified MD2 class O & K four wheel diesel locomotive also appeared in the Clearance photograph album, which could also have belonged to the Sudan PWD. These locomotives were fitted with a 22 h.p. twin cylinder engine and three-speed gear box with chain drive to the rear axle. As this particular class of locomotive was only introduced in about 1934, the Sudan locomotive may well have been supplied new for the sand clearance job, but as surviving O & K diesel locomotive production records are incomplete for this period, no positive identification has been possible.

Wagons on the Tokar Sand Clearance

The 1938 PWD Annual Report referred to 350 tip wagons and 50 five cubic metre capacity wagons being delivered for use on the Clearance, a considerable fleet. Amongst many V-skips shown in the Clearance album there were slight variations in bucket shape, indicating that they almost certainly came from different builders. The five cubic metre wagons were of three designs, all apparently descended from the WDLR "D" class. One all-steel design had two half-length drop doors on each side, with what looked like steel box section reinforcing the tops of sides and ends. A second design resembled the "D" class more closely, with wooden planked half-length doors, but with two pronounced vertical angle irons strengthening the outside of each door. The sides looked to be higher than the 2ft of the "D" class. Both these designs had bogies which protruded beyond the end of the wagon bodies (WDLR-style) and flat "V" shaped bracing below the main chassis solebars, as on the "D" class. A third, all-steel design had high, partially rounded ends and pronounced angle iron reinforcing, both vertically and diagonally, on the outsides of half-length steel doors. The bogies of this design were completely beneath the body. No further details of these wagons have as yet been discovered.

Chapter 12

ALTERNATIVE LINKS FROM TOKAR
TO THE RED SEA COAST

During 1871, the year when the first rail link between Tokar and Trinkitat was proposed, Hill noted that Khedive [Ismail] asked Johann Werner Munzinger Bey, the Swiss Governor of Massawa, to report on work needed to develop Trinkitat as a port. Munzinger also reported on the possibility of port development at Aqiq, some 80 kilometres southeast of Trinkitat, where he found "the best [deep-water] harbour on the Red Sea coast". He recommended building a railway into the interior which would have eventually reached the regional centre of Kassala, some 400 kilometres inland. The relevance of that scheme to our story, as Hill noted, is that a 19 kilometre branch line was proposed to serve "the Tokar cotton plantation". Nothing more seems to have been heard of plans to develop a major port at Aqiq.

However, the Tokar cotton crop was primarily destined for ginneries at Suakin and Port Sudan. Why, then, were direct overland routes – by rail or road – not preferred to the more cumbersome process of transport firstly by light railway to Trinkitat, then onwards by sea? Taking rail first, the 3ft 6in. gauge line from Suakin towards Tokar, proposed from Kitchener's time onwards, never quite gained sufficient priority to be actually laid down. When rail routes from the coast to the Nile were being planned at the turn of the century, surveyors considered a trace from Suakin southwards along Kitchener's route through Tokar to Kassala, then westwards towards Khartoum, but finally favoured the more direct route to the Nile at Atbara, opened in 1905.

Hill noted two later occasions when it was seriously proposed to build a 3ft 6in. gauge branch line from the Red Sea Railway near Suakin to Tokar, specifically to bring out the cotton crop. In 1911, the Governor General of the Sudan, Sir Reginald Wingate, expressed the hope that it would not be long before money was available to extend the railway to Tokar. He was confident that it would not only pay for itself but expand trade. No further progress was made at that time, but in July 1919, Sir Edward Midwinter, the SR General Manager, announced that the Government had approved in principle the extension of the Suakin branch line to Tokar, a distance of 100km. [about 60ml.]. A token half-kilometre of track was laid southwards from Shata station (close to Suakin), but Hill recorded that the project was shelved due to the prohibitive post-war cost of rails and sleepers. The TTLR, built soon after, was to be the "temporary expedient" which lasted until road transport fully took over the cotton crop in the 1950s. An important 3ft. 6in. line southwards from the Red Sea Railway towards Kassala was laid down in the 1920s, thus achieving the overall objectives of both

Munzinger and Kitchener. However, it branched off at Haiya Junction, well to the west of Tokar, and did not serve the cotton growing district of the Khor Baraka delta.

Road transport had also been considered. Williams thought that the TTLR was "a highly contentious light railway" because it brought the SR and himself into conflict with Provincial officials. Instead of using the TTLR, they wanted the Tokar cotton crop taken "... by lorry to Suakin, over the punishing road, with the resulting wear and tear on vehicles... The road from Port Sudan to Suakin was good, but its continuation southwards to Tokar was not. It ran over the coastal plain, and the last half was through 30 foot high sand dunes, which were difficult to negotiate without local skill, it was always a very difficult ride... The Province officials wanted the lorries, and set the haulage rates to cover the enormous cost of spares needed. We [Sudan Railways] were against inflicting spares shortages on the country as a whole, and favoured use of the facilities already provided by light railway and sea transport. We generally won the argument." Despite William's championship of the TTLR, it was the lorries (albeit privately owned), aided by the ever-present camels, which finally won the argument.

At about the same time as the TTLR closed in 1952, services on the line from Sallom Junction to Suakin – long since reduced to branch line status, with the main line running to Port Sudan – also ceased. The Sudan Railways entry in "World Railways 1954-55" included the simple statement:

"The branch line from Sallom to Suakin and the narrow gauge line between Trinkitat and Tokar have been dismantled."

REFERENCES

Anon, 1885. Inventions Exhibition – Swivel Bogie Locomotive. The Engineer, 31 July 1885, pp 82-84.

Anon, 1933. Diesel locomotives for the Sudan Government (Hawthorn Leslie diesels). Reprinted from Supplement to The Railway Gazette, 24 February 1933.

Anon, 1938? Tokar Sand Clearance, 1937 1938. Presented by K. B. el Koussa, contractor, to Mr B. Kennedy Cook, M.C., Governor, Kassala. An album of 163 photographs. In the Sudan Archive, University of Durham.

Anon, 1953. Diesel Operation in The Sudan (Sudan Gezira Board's railway). Diesel Railway Traction, Vol. 7, No. 258, November 1953, pp 245/6.

Anon, 1962. The Railway Bridge of the Silvery Tay and Other Disasters. Selected from the Works of William McGonagall. 1962 edition (originally published by David Winter and Son Ltd), Sphere Books, London.

Anon, 1993. More on the Khartoum steam trams. Continental Railway Journal, No. 96, Winter 1993/94, pp 453-455.

Anon, 1994. Summary guide to the Sudan Archive (1994 edition). Durham University Library, Durham.

Anon, 1998. Eritrea news report. Continental Railway Journal, No. 113, Spring 1998, p 139.

Arnott, G., 1973. Army 240. Industrial Railway Record, No. 50, October 1973, pp 109-111.

Baker, Allan C., 1985. The first hundred Bagnalls. Industrial Railway Record, No. 100, February 1985, pp 218-258.

Baker, Allan C. and Civil, T. D. Allen, 1973. Bagnalls of Stafford. The Oakwood Press, Lingfield, Surrey.

Baker, Allan C. and Civil, T. D. Allen, 1984. Bagnalls of Stafford, locomotive works list. The Industrial Locomotive Society, Richmond, Surrey.

Bennett, John, 1987. The Khartoum steam trams. Continental Railway Journal, No. 72, Winter 1987/88, pp 364-367.

Bishop, Dennis, and Davies, W. J. K., 1972. Railways and war before 1918. Blandford Press, London.

Bowen, R. A., Kalla-Bishop, P. M., and Lera N., 1976. Railways of Ethiopia – 1. Northern Ethiopia Railway. Continental Railway Journal, No. 27, Autumn 1976, pp 16/17.

Bowen, R. A., Kalla-Bishop, P. M., and Lera N., 1977. Railways of Ethiopia – 2. Northern Ethiopia Railway (continued, including locomotive list). Continental Railway Journal, No. 29, Spring 1977, pp 90/91.

Brown, A. Samler, and Brown, G. Gordon (Eds.), 1914. The guide to South and East Africa for the use of tourists, sportsmen, invalids and settlers (for the Union-Castle Mail Steamship Co. Ltd.) (twentieth edition). Samson Low, Marston, London.

Browning, John, 1995. A military mystery tour. Industrial Railway Record, No. 141, June 1995, pp 473-480; plus correspondence in No. 146, September 1996, pp 218-219.

Clarke, Brian R. and Veitch, Christopher C., 1986. The eighteen inch gauge Royal Arsenal Railway at Woolwich. Brian R. Clarke, Bath, Avon.

Davies, W. J. K., 1967. Light railways of the First World War. David & Charles, Newton Abbot, Devon.

Eliot, T. S. (Ed.), 1941. A choice of Kipling's verse. Faber & Faber, London.

Fricke, K., Bude, R. and Murray, M., 1978. Orenstein & Koppel Steam Locomotives Works List, 1892-1945. Arley Hall Publications.

Gleichen, Lt.-Col. Count (Ed.), 1905. The Anglo-Egyptian Sudan: A compendium prepared by officers of the Sudan Government. Volume I (Geographical, Descriptive and Historical); Volume II (Routes.). His Majesty's Stationery Office, London.

Gratton, Robert and Band, Stuart R., 1989. The Ashover Light Railway. Wild Swan, Didcot, Oxfordshire.

Heritage, T. R., 1999. The Light Track from Arras. (Second edition.) Plateway Press, East Harling, Norfolk.

Hill, Richard, 1965. Sudan Transport – A history of railway, marine and river services in the Republic of the Sudan. Oxford University Press, London.

Hill, Richard, 1987. Gordon: Yet another assessment. Sudan Studies Society of the United Kingdom, London.

Hughes, D. N. R. (Ed.), 1974. Guide to the Leighton Buzzard Narrow Gauge Railway (second edition). LBNGR Society, Leighton Buzzard, Bedfordshire.

The Hydrographer to the Navy. Admiralty Chart No. 675 (of or including) Trinkitat Harbour. Various editions from 1885 to 1988. Held at the United Kingdom Hydrographic Office, Taunton, Somerset.

The Hydrographer to the Navy. Red Sea Pilot. Various editions from 1900 to 1944. Held at the United Kingdom Hydographic Office, Taunton, Somerset.

Jewell, John H. A., 1969. Dhows at Mombasa. East African Publishing House, Nairobi, Kenya.

Kunhardt, Capt. H G, 1885a. Notes on the Suakin-Berber Railway. The Royal Engineers Journal, July 1, 1885, pp 155/6.

Kunhardt, Capt. H G, 1885b. Narrow gauge locomotives. The Royal Engineers Journal, December 1, 1885, p 273.

Moorhead, Alan, 1960. The White Nile. 1963 edition (originally published by Hamish Hamilton, London), Penguin Books, Harmondsworth, Middlesex.

Motor Rail Ltd., 1932. A catalogue of "Simplex" Internal Combustion Locomotives. Republished by the Moseley Railway Trust, August 2000.

Nutting, Anthony, 1966. Gordon, martyr and misfit. 1967 edition (originally published by Constable, London), The Reprint Society edition, London.

Pole, F. J. C. and Smith, Roger T., 1924. Report on Sudan Government Railways and Steamers, January 1924. Paddington Station, London.

Pole, Sir Felix J. C., 1931. Second Report on Sudan Government Railways, January 1931. Paddington Station, London.

Porter, D. M. Two pages of a photographic album. In the Sudan Archive, University of Durham.

Robertson, Leslie S., 1898. Narrow gauge railways, two feet and under. Originally published in the Proceedings of the Institution of Civil Engineers. 1988 edition, with additional material and a new introduction by Andrew Neale, Plateway Press, Croydon, Surrey.

Robinson, Capt. W. W., 1885. Narrow gauge locomotives. The Royal Engineers Journal, August 1, 1885, pp 182/3.

Sampson, Henry (Ed.), 1955. World Railways 1954–55. Sampson Low's "World Railways" Ltd., London.

Sharp, D. L., 1945. The Tokar Trinkitat Light Railway. The Sudan Railway Bulletin, No. 81, September 1945, p 3.

Smith, D. H. and Down C. G., 1979. Brockham Museum Guide. Brockham Museum Association, Haywards Heath, Sussex.

Smithers, Mark, 1992. Camden Fort. The Narrow Gauge, No. 136, Autumn 1992, p 31.

Smithers, Mark, 1993. An illustrated history of 18 inch gauge steam railways. Oxford Publishing Co., Sparkford, Somerset.

Storrar, G. R. Diaries of life in the Sudan (handwritten, with photographs inserted). In the Sudan Archive, University of Durham.

Sudan Public Works Department. Annual Report for 1938. Khartoum.

Sudan Railways and predecessors. Annual Reports for 1924, 1929, 1932 and 1937. Atbara.

Taylorson, Keith, 1987. Narrow gauge at war. Plateway Press, Croydon, Surrey.

Taylorson, Keith, Narrow gauge at war – 2. Plateway Press, Brighton, Sussex.

Thomas, H. B. and Scott, Robert, 1935. Uganda. Oxford University Press, London.

Webb, Brian, 1973. The British internal-combustion locomotive: 1894-1940. David and Charles, Newton Abbot, Devon.

West, Roger, 1981. RENOWN. Industrial Railway Record, No. 90, September 1981, pp 334-337.

Williams, C. R., 1986. Wheels and paddles in the Sudan 1923–1946. The Pentland Press, Kippielaw, Scotland.

Wylde, A. B., 1888. '83 to '87 in the Sudan: with an account of Sir William Hewett's mission to King John of Abyssinia. Remington, London.

NOTES ON THE AUTHOR

After working as a volunteer on the restoration of the Welshpool and Llanfair Light Railway through the 1960s, Henry Gunston started to work overseas in 1968. His job in water resources research took him first to Kenya, Uganda and Tanzania, where he started a life-long interest in the railways in those countries. In the mid 1970s he worked for a year in Ecuador, where steam trains worked on incredible 1 in 18 grades.

Regular visits to Sri Lanka, where he took a special interest in the 2ft 6in. gauge Kelani Valley Railway, were followed by a return to Kenya for three years in the mid 1980s. He has an engineering degree and has written a number of articles on the history of the railways in countries he has visited.

The Railway World of
PLATEWAY PRESS

UK PUBLIC RAILWAYS

The West Clare Railway

The Dingle Train

The Rye and Camber Tramway – A Centenary History

Ratty – A History of the Ravenglass and Eskdale Railway

The Surrey Border and Camberley Railway

The Campbeltown & Machrihanish Light Railway

INDUSTRIAL GWYNEDD

Industrial Gwynedd – Volume 2, 1997

Industrial Gwynedd – Volume 3, 1998

Industrial Gwynedd – Volume 4, 1999

WORLD RAILWAYS

Narrow Gauge Railways of Portugal

Minor Railways of France

Railways of the Andes

Mountain Railways and Locomotives from Old Picture Postcards

The Narrow Gauge Railways of Spain:

Volume 1 – Catalunya to the Sierra Nevada

Volume 2 – Castile to the Biscay Coast

The Two Foot Gauge Enigma – Beira Railway 1890-1900

Clouds on the Brienzer Rothorn – A short history of the Brienz Rothorn Railway

Narrow Gauge Rails to Esquel

MILITARY RAILWAYS

Narrow Gauge at War – Volume 2

The Light Track from Arras

Fortress Railways of the Baltic Shores

The RAF Masirah Railway